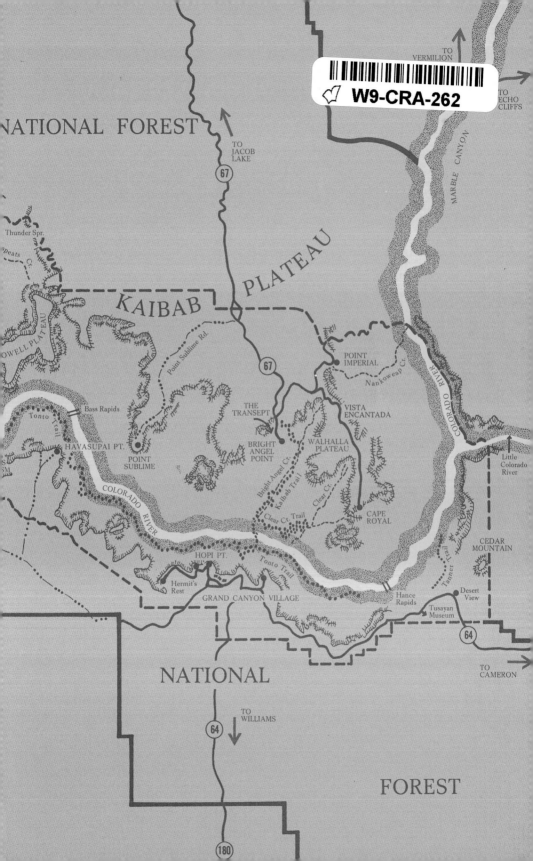

THE WILDERNESS WORLD
of the
GRAND CANYON

"Leave it as it is"

THE WILDERNESS WORLD
of the
GRAND CANYON

"Leave it as it is"

Ann and Myron Sutton

Photographs by Philip Hyde

J. B. Lippincott Company · *Philadelphia* · *New York*
1971

To Goldie Marie Sutton,
without whose inspiration the Grand Canyon
—and life itself—
would have had less meaning.

Foreword

THE ADVICE OF Theodore Roosevelt that every American ought to see the Grand Canyon remained good for about fifty years. He made that statement in 1903, the era in which hotels were first built at the edge, the first automobiles arrived on the rim, and tourists began to show up at the rate of perhaps a hundred a year.

He meant, of course, that every American would be immensely proud of his country if he gazed into this superlative portion of it, would be thrilled by the beauty and solitude, and would be refreshed in spirit—perhaps even humbled a bit—by the grandeur and antiquity of the scene.

However, if every American today tried to visit the Grand Canyon, there might not be much of its solitude left. If all citizens of other countries, who are entitled to equal rights, were to visit it, we would have on our hands a crisis of some importance. Even at the current rate of two million visits annually, the Canyon is in trouble, and year after year the challenges grow more complex and more difficult to meet.

Few of them require technological solution, which is the major way man has learned to solve his problems. These challenges facing him at the Grand Canyon revolve around simple things, like joy and gladness, quiet, clean air, the lives of animals, a tree in bloom.

All these are perishable. They are also introductory to the Colorado Plateau, which is made up of thousands of sights and sounds, and they help realign man's understanding of what the Grand Canyon is.

As a geologic phenomenon, it contains a superb collection of fossils, rocks, and terrestrial evidence of the earth in motion. As a scenic attraction, it captures the eye with color, form, and startling immensity.

Were these all, we could render Roosevelt's dictum true and open the gorge to all humanity.

But the Canyon happens to be in a national park—and that changes nearly everything. That confers upon this gorge a greater totality than rocks and fossils and colors. Parks are for animals as well as for rocks, for plants as well as for rainbows, and every living organism has a niche in the total system. Each element of the environment has been fitted precisely to its present position and its present function.

Even so, man's idea of a national park is still evolving. In such a place, he now discovers, the sky and silence take on greater importance than anywhere else. Whatever has nourished the pristine wilderness through millenniums of evolution should still be there, including the absence of *Homo sapiens.*

Human beings have not always known the meaning of silence, and perhaps wouldn't now had they not been so deprived of it in urban and suburban environments, and did they not need it so badly in national parks.

This book goes as deeply as we know how—from forty years' combined experience in and around the Canyon and from studying national parks in twenty countries—into some of the forgotten reasons why the Grand Canyon is a national park. Our aims include the sharing of joys it has been our pleasure to experience there: the glories of a winter hike; the thrill of being caught in a summer storm, of listening to an orchestra of wind through the pines at dusk; the call of a coyote; the celestial song of a hermit thrush; the echoing notes of canyon wrens in an amphitheater fit for gods. . . .

What music there is! Or was.

We go behind the scenes to survey the human management of a vastly complex inhuman system and to see how grave are the threats to this area, this solitude, this music. We study the management policies men have fashioned to keep the Canyon unimpaired and try to show where these are inadequate or difficult to apply. And finally we review some possible answers to some difficult questions.

In a larger sense we ask whether men have saved the wonders of this nation through sacrifice and battle against obvious opposition only to lose what they won through subtle or uncontrollable damage. The Grand Canyon is a case in point, because of all the American heritage it seems the least destructible. It is not. It is vulnerable in hidden ways. It is not a renewable resource. Another will not grow in its place.

Much attention has been focused on the threat of dam construction that would inundate portions of the Canyon, and it is well to stave off the setting of precedents. But what if, with our attention diverted to other efforts, something more serious happens to the whole Canyon?

We touch the geology, ecology, history, archeology, and scenery of the Canyon, and draw upon special words of beauty and wisdom that have been written about it. We consider the meaning of the Canyon, and identify the role it plays in the national as well as international structure of national parks and equivalent reserves.

After all, it is a wonderful, majestic, incredible Canyon, full of inspiration, full of lessons for all, full of beauty and spectacle, but imperiled and deserving of constant surveillance by the public at large—as a flawless diamond deserves great care and safeguarding.

This book is not intended to sustain any side of any argument, sharpen contentions, rebuke, or summarize controversies. Instead, we explore the Canyon and ideas of how it can be conserved and used in the changing times of today and tomorrow.

Among every set of ideas, to be sure, are those that seem impractical or unnecessary. Yet in the seventies man must keep alive his thinking of how to handle threats to the national heritage. This is especially true in the national park system, 94 per cent of which is devoted to areas primarily of natural significance.

Perhaps when we hand the Canyon over to our children in the eighties, and they to theirs after that, there will still be in the Canyon something of that primeval wonder about which John Wesley Powell once wrote: "It is the land of music."

Ann and Myron Sutton
Alexandria, Virginia

Acknowledgments

To THE SUPERINTENDENTS AND STAFFS of Grand Canyon National Park we owe a debt of gratitude for many years of guidance, suggestions, insights, and introductions to the joys of the trailside, the rim forests, the desert floor, and the river. We discussed modern management problems with the park staff and the manuscript has benefited immeasurably from their review. Officials of the Washington office of the National Park Service have also been most helpful in erasing misconceptions, and we are deeply grateful for every courtesy and assistance.

The National Park Service, however, is not accountable for statements and policy interpretations herein; official documents and booklets available to the public cover policies in detail. We prefer to consider policy with an open mind, to study the public judgment of it, set the Canyon in perspective, see where it fits in the fabric of human society, suggest, assess, enter new fields perhaps—not to attack, condemn, or bewail.

We also would like to thank the Havasupai Tribe, the Bureau of Indian Affairs, the Museum of Northern Arizona, the regional office of the National Park Service in Santa Fe, New Mexico, and the staff of the Horace M. Albright Training Center at the Grand Canyon for assistance rendered.

Special thanks go to Dr. Agnes M. Allen of Northern Arizona University for many years of competent, untiring guidance into the fields of geology, geography, and public land administration. District Ranger John Riffey of Grand Canyon National Monument spared no effort to see that we saw and understood his faraway corner of the Colorado Plateau. Philip Hyde offered many insights into man's

Acknowledgments

appreciation—or lack of it—for wild lands. George Stevens, Robert D. Mead, and Betty Jane Corson have given good counsel throughout. To all of these persons we are grateful beyond our ability to say.

Dr. Harvey Butchart, who has doubtless hiked more of the Grand Canyon than any man alive, provided unforgettable hiking inspiration in years gone by and helped to teach us the forms of the art. To Frank F. Kowski we owe special gratitude for many hours of patient explanation of national-park history and policy from his long and wide understanding of it.

Michael and Larry Sutton, who manned the machines by which we taped and photographed the wonders of the Canyon for detailed recollection, and who hiked the trails and roamed the forests with patience and understanding, have our lasting appreciation.

We should like to pay special credit to Louis Schellbach, who for more than twenty years occupied with high distinction the position of park naturalist at Grand Canyon National Park. In that capacity he gave to thousands of persons a profound introduction to the spirit of man, the wonders of the Canyon, and the values of all nature.

"Our lives are so short," he used to say. "But if we appreciate and understand natural things, we will be living more lives than one."

Ann and Myron Sutton

Contents

1

HIDDEN RIVER

THE HORSES were ready at dawn. Deep snow covered the landscape, lay on the trees, and spilled over the edge of the Canyon. As the sun rose, the temperature stood exactly at zero.

Rapidly a blue-white world became a yellow one. The sun appeared on the horizon like a burning coal. It enlarged. Its rays struck out across the snow, widened, expanded, engulfed the scraggly pinyon pines, and illuminated the steam from our breaths as volcanic clouds are lighted by subterranean fires.

Horses stood almost to the stirrups in powdered whiteness, awaiting the signal to start. The food, cooking gear, and sleeping bags on their backs received a final check.

We hoisted our own packs to our shoulders.

"Your last chance to turn back, Doctor."

He smiled, looking ludicrous in a shapeless olive coat and ear-hugging cap. His slender nose was red, the eyes but slits, the demeanor of the surgeon disappearing as he clapped his ears and stamped a place in the snow.

But he said nothing. He was ready to go.

At the rim we stopped. The deeps below still lay in shadow. Silence pervaded the scene. The cloak of snow absorbed almost every sound, yet the thinness of the air, here on the south rim at 7,000 feet, and its sharpness, brilliance, and clarity seemed to convey the slightest of the noises that did exist.

The distant call of a Steller's jay filtered through the woods, and whenever we took off our caps or ear muffs, we could detect the faint sound of a clump of snow falling from one of the trees some distance away, first sign of the coming warmth.

All the trees lay covered, almost buried. Their sunny sides looked like a billowing collection of clouds, the shadowed sides like bluish-white cloaks of nuns.

The Canyon itself seemed to be a white layer cake with red frosting separating the tiers. The sun had begun to illumine the higher, more yellowish layers as well as tips of a few high buttes within. The rest lay subdued in shadow.

The lower half of the gorge was free of snow, or nearly so. The bottom, dark with shadow, seemed lifeless, silent, and cold.

We did not watch very long, lest time get away. We had seventeen miles to hike, and these February days were short.

One by one, the five of us, wrapped in jackets and ear muffs, shod in high boots, adorned with packs, went over the edge and down the steeply pitching grade of the Kaibab (rhymes with "high lab") Trail. The two horses, one to carry bedding and food, the other saddled for human transport if that became necessary, stumbled as we did, step by laborious step in three feet of snow.

We had driven the night before from Flagstaff, a hundred miles by road across the high Arizona plateaus. For weeks we had planned the trip as a kind of getaway from the work or study that held each of us to a rigid routine. Bonds of friendship united the group—friendship and a love of the great outdoors. Now that we were on the trail, our hearts were light, our spirits free.

We slipped. We slid. We staggered against rock ledges. It did little good to watch where we put our feet, for the snow hid rocks and ridges, or it concealed erosion channels into which we plunged almost to the hips.

No sun brightened the abyss below the rim. The only light came from a pale blue morning sky and the slowly reddening cliffs below, seen through silhouettes of trees that hugged the steep talus slopes or sheer rock walls.

It was not difficult to fall behind the rest of the group. A scene so clean and pure compelled admiration. Shapes and shadows presented an admirable gallery of art, architecture, and sculpture—part traditional, part contemporary, all spontaneous. With every step the shapes either changed or dissolved, and always took on new effects of lighting.

Another pinnacle. A different wall. A new alcove. No matter how

2

Winter settles over yucca, grass, and pinyon pine.

many trips we had made before, there were a thousand new things to see.

The edge of the cliff above, yellowed in morning light, looked like the steep stair steps of a Theban temple. The tops of the pinnacles, their rocks rounded off and covered with snow, seemed as though they were monkeys in white caps laughing at our struggles.

We were worth laughing at—captives of gravity and prisoners in the snow. The lower portion of the doctor's long coat had turned white where it had been dragging through the snowy powder. Once he looked back, but only briefly, as though to say: "Cheyava had better be worth it."

The Kolb Brothers, Emory and Ellsworth, those daring and persistent Canyon explorers, had come upon Cheyava Falls in 1903 and explored it, marveling at its 1,000-foot height, lowering themselves down the cliff, and entering a large cave behind it, a cave that they said measured sixty feet high and three hundred feet deep. Believing the flow of water to be intermittent, they had given it the Hopi Indian word *cheyava*, meaning "off and on."

Cheyava Falls lay so distant and deeply hidden that few people, as far as we knew, had ever seen them. They lay over there, somewhere, below the opposite rim of the canyon, where no trail reached.

We had talked with the chief ranger of Grand Canyon National Park about it when we informed him of our intended route. He had never been there but he knew of the falls. Topographic maps of the United States Geological Survey showed Cheyava Falls on the right-hand fork of Clear Creek, but the chief ranger allowed that that must be a mistake. According to information he had, the falls were up the left-hand fork. As this advice seemed up to date, we had decided to follow it.

Down the switchbacks, zigzagging back and forth in the dark recesses below the rim, we came to where the trail straightened out and passed beneath a 300-foot cliff of Kaibab limestone, shaded and north facing. As the other members of the party had by now moved far ahead, there seemed no longer to be other living creatures in the world. At such times a hiker feels a curious sense of release.

The squeaking leather of pack straps, the slight clanking sound of whatever had not been packed as well as it should were happy, familiar sounds. Once came a voice from below, testing the echo propensities of the Canyon cliffs. That, too, was a happy sound, and it was probably the doctor's. Now, at last, he could unbend. Tradition bound him so tightly in the community that he seldom felt able to release his spirit and shout as he had when a boy.

Here, all those things became possible, even acceptable. He could go without shaving and nobody cared. He could say whatever he pleased—and he did. He was free.

We were all free!

We had been granted the most glorious of days. Our powers seemed inadequate to the challenge of making full use of so lavish a gift, but we would use it as well and as much as possible.

Urban images and city sounds lay far above and behind. Here everything was sharp and clear. Here everything came into focus.

And here we came to reaffirm the one great fact of the Canyon land. It was a quiet land. The trees, the cliffs, the very gorge itself made no noise save for some imagined hollow breath of hugeness, perhaps an industrial illusion derived from the thought that anything so big must make some kind of noise.

The migratory birds were far away. No swallows or swifts flew over the edge or dived and swooped among the trees. Rock squirrels and chipmunks must have been in their burrows, for we neither heard nor saw them.

The spell was so perfect and the totality of things so marvelously held together that we quickly became a part of the Canyon environment.

The farther down we went, the less deep the snow became. As we descended more switchbacks through the Coconino sandstone and strode out of the shadows onto a promontory that jutted into the open air, we forgot every confinement of civilization.

We had entered a world in which we were masters of our thoughts, but happily mastered and conquered by the immensity around us. We wanted nothing to change it—no sound of horn or engine or whistle, no shrill of siren, no ring of telephone. . . .

Quiet, a rare commodity, overwhelmed us.

Free of the enclosing walls, we shortly found ourselves in an open valley rather than the steep-walled canyon that this gorge appeared to be when viewed from above. The rim from which we had started lay 1,000 feet up and behind. Across to the north rim, nearly ten miles away, the trees seemed small, the snow but a delicate crust.

By now little snow lay on the trail, only a slush that slowly melted. Not only was the day growing warmer, but we were descending

A mantle of white reaches almost to the lowest depths.

into a desert environment where average temperatures ranged from 15 to 20 degrees higher than on the rim.

Buttes that earlier had merged with the background of the opposite rim became detached and presented themselves in profile. The gorge assumed more understandable dimensions. We were able to use ourselves as a yardstick to measure it because we were engulfed by it.

The snow, as we went on, became mixed with red Hermit shale, and our boots and trousers took on a covering of rich red mud.

Suddenly we stopped. An old juniper leaned over the trail. The early sun had just reached it. Golden light reflected from its bare gray trunk, and the few places where reddish fibers remained threw back a vivid rusty color. The western sky, deepened in blue as the morning proceeded, showed through the twisted branches. Clusters of scaly leaves seemed awkwardly placed, yet there was something compelling about the arrangement, the forms, the shadows, the matching of colors.

The other members of the party were getting farther ahead. They would be waiting at the fossil quarry. They would be impatient. Another sixteen miles remained.

We had to pass a number of simple, familiar things beside the trail: a clump of grass, some ancient rain pits in the sandstone, old cross-bedded planes in the cliffs, the prickly pears, empty skeletons of single-leaf ash. We would see them all again.

Our steps quickened. The mud and slush slowed us down, caused us to slip, compelled us to watch the trail rather than the drama unfolding all around.

When we joined the others, the doctor looked upon us with a bit more kindness, relieved as he was of the burden of hiking through snow. He glanced at the rim, still cold and glistening, from which we had come, then gave a mock shudder, turned and went on down the trail.

Rapidly the temperature rose above freezing, though the sharp and bracing air still caused our faces to tingle. Here and there the junipers framed a rich and colorful scene, but the farther we descended, the fewer the junipers became, until at last we ran out of them altogether.

The sun grew brighter as it climbed in the sky, and its energy seemed to rejuvenate tiring muscles.

Time disappeared. We neither knew nor cared whether it was eight o'clock or ten. If hunger came, we snacked on dried peaches (which the doctor considered a nadir of tastelessness but which took on a welcome flavor so far from civilization).

Time had no meaning. The sun would climb to the zenith and then descend. Dusk would come. Night would fall. These would be the only landmarks of the day. To make Clear Creek by dusk, we had to watch the movement not of hands on a watch but of sun in the sky. Only the sun would tell us whether we were making slow or rapid progress. And the sun was no taskmaster. It would shine benevolently whether our steps were too fast or too slow. It could not curse us if we delayed, fire us if we dallied, or prod us if we stopped too many times.

Our legs were getting a little sore, our hips a little pained from the constant pounding. That didn't matter. Nothing mattered but the spacious freedom and the silent spell of nearly primeval wilderness.

Down, down, down. The world became a void, and we sank into it. The trail cut down through gray marble rocks of Redwall limestone, switching back and forth. The sun glared. Sheer walls reared massively hundreds of feet above.

The trail became less steep, dry now and almost dusty. Before we knew it we had arrived at the edge of the inner gorge.

Now we could hear the roar of the Colorado River 1,500 feet below, swirling ponderously from one granite crag to another, carrying stones with a rumbling voice along its bed, curling into a thousand whirlpools, breaking now and then into white rapids.

The doctor and the rest of the party waved from far below, and we moved quickly to catch up. Beneath the hard rock cliffs our steps became faster. A knifelike ridge of Hakatai shale compelled a pause, for there seemed in all this canyon of colors nothing so fine and reddish-orange. Never had a trip into this gorge been so rapid that we could not stop to examine anew the texture, the color, the antiquity of this simple shale.

Had heaven a stairway of marble, it could hardly be more pleasing to the eye than this. On ancient Proterozoic deltas, some 600 million years ago, these muds had been deposited and baked; time had turned them to stone. The river had since eroded and revealed them. It all appeared so orderly in a gorge where chaos seemed to reign, where no cliff, no layer, no crevice looked born of order. Yet a continuity did exist, perhaps part of the strange continuity of the universe.

It may seem rather strange that a human being can have a fondness and affection for a layer of rock, but it happens, and perhaps only geologists can understand. Such was our case with the Hakatai shale,

9

and only with reluctance did we tear away and go on down the trail.

Jackets had along ago been loosened, removed, then strung on the belt. The temperature must have been 60 degrees. Such daily variation between dawn and midday is not uncommon in Southwestern winters.

The trail steepened again. The music and rhythmic beat of boot against rock sent echoes among the walls. Around the bends, into and out of cool shadows, past granite walls and black rock coves, through the tunnel, across the suspension bridge, along the opposite side of the river, and we arrived at Phantom Ranch.

A ranch, even this one, replete with buildings, fences, corrals and swimming pool, seemed incongruous and irrelevant to our needs. We came self-reliant and, besides, did not want to lose the spell of wildness that had overtaken us on the downward trek.

So with only the briefest of rests, the morning half gone and nine miles to hike, we hoisted our packs again and set off up Bright Angel Creek.

A few hundred yards from the last of the buildings, a less well-maintained trail branched off sharply to the right and started up steeply.

Now we were climbing. At first it came as a shock; unused muscles strained in complaint. We slowed down. The doctor knelt and crawled along the trail on hands and knees. We laughed at him and ourselves.

Up and out of the inner gorge we came, stepping over rocks that lay tumbled in the trail. Or onto narrow ledges above the river, next to open spaces extending a thousand feet or more to the wide brown waters below.

As we came out on the Tonto Platform, into the openness again, clouds appeared over both the rims. A few moments later we lost the light of the sun. The good weather was not to last. The temperature dropped, and our jackets went on again.

Once again we lagged behind. The ledges, the cactus, the sounds of animals we could neither see nor identify—even in winter the canyon had a great deal to tell and a great many mysteries.

In the quiet it seemed blasphemous even to scrape our boots on the rocks. Man-sounds became so small and trifling where everything was so immense. The forward-jutting cliff of Sumner Point loomed overhead like the prow of a giant battleship such as men had never

10

Sun-specked ripples on Bright Angel Creek.

built or as it might look to fishermen on a skiff in its path. Everything seemed a hundred times larger than life.

A wall, a promontory, another point, a monolith. Suddenly the gorge seemed like a cathedral, a temple, a shrine, something beyond price, something sacred.

Over there—an altar. And there a narthex. And yonder a steeple, then many steeples, and more behind. Along the wall at our left, and the one across the canyon opposite, were alcoves. What giant candles they would hold! Windows, ledges, columns, a thousand statues— but not a gargoyle among them, a shepherd, not an eagle. If there were eagles here, they would be live ones, on free wings.

Many times we stumbled that morning for having taken our eyes from the trail to scan the cliffs and alcoves and steeples. Snowflakes began to fall, their icy touch a tingle to the cheek. They swirled across the Tonto Platform, into shadows and out, blowing in swarms, changing course and coming directly at us, stinging, biting, freezing.

Clouds poured into the gorge, black or gray, lighted with shafts of sunlight, curling and plunging as a wave does when it strikes the shore, only to be jostled and crowded and pushed this way and that in ceaseless motion. All this in turn produced a herd of shadows that galloped across the gentle plain, or plunged directly over the cliffs and fell into the gorge, or clawed their way up the cliffs, ran madly along the slopes and climbed diagonally over red rock faces as though they were fleeing other shadows that came up out of the inner gorge in cold and silent pursuit.

Both rims had gone. The tops of temples were now obscured. Yet so much remained to see that our eyes could not move fast enough to take in all the scene at once, or even to follow more than one of the hundred dramas being performed. We turned around, and even dared to walk a few steps backward, trying not to miss anything. But it was no use.

If we are to be hikers in the next world, God grant us eyes in the back of the head.

We had lunch on a ledge that day. We built a small fire and heated cans of meat, and the hot food felt fine inside. It was good to relax, too, and exchange experiences with the rest of the party, so strung out had we been all morning.

All too soon, lunch break was over. We had to be at Clear Creek before dark, and not even the sun could tell us the time now. The trail had no signposts, no mileage markers, no intersections. We were on our own. And we had to move.

Sumner Point receded in the distance and Bradley Point loomed above. Light flurries of pelting hard-frozen snow raced across the black-brush flats; gusts hurled them into the vegetation or picked them up again and thrust them into the sky.

By late afternoon we began to grow weary. We had covered fifteen miles of winding rocky trail, had dropped nearly 5,000 feet in elevation, climbed a part of that back, and at times driven ourselves against icy winds.

But the sun came out again, buoying our spirits. It was sinking toward the horizon now; the day would soon be over. Light spilled across the great gray cliff beneath which we walked. Talus slopes, one after another, lay along the base of the cliff, and we started going around them.

"How soon?" the doctor asked.

We had no way of knowing. Finally we arrived at the gorge in whose depths lay Clear Creek, but the tributary canyon held its secrets too far below to be seen. At this point we turned and made our way along the west rim of it, around the multiple talus slopes.

"How far?" the doctor asked.

We had no reply, except "Around the next bend."

But around each bend was another and then another.

After a while the doctor no longer believed—none of us believed—that the trail would ever end. We were wearied to the bone; tired; exhausted; sleepy; the muscles of shoulders and back now sore. It seemed as though the curving trail would go on forever and we would simply disintegrate and turn into stones along the trailside as perhaps others hikers had done before us.

The rest of that day remains obscure and hazy in memory. Somehow the last bend was rounded, somehow there was a long steep slope, and then Clear Creek came into view.

The sight of so crystal and pure a stream would awaken anyone, 13 and the taste of it, cold and sharp, brought us to life at once. We made camp, pulled a dozen trout from the water, cooked them and ate.

By firelight we studied the map to scout out the next day's route. After that we lost no time rolling out the sleeping bags and getting into them.

Numbed by the jogging on the trail and lulled by a thousand images that filtered through the brain, we lay there, looking up at the stars, now bright in a clear sky, and waited for sleep to blot them out.

That didn't take long.

The next day dawned perfectly clear. With slowly opening eyes we glimpsed the glistening white trees on the north rim, so magnified in the brilliance that they seemed almost touchable.

Not a crystal of snow had melted up there. The trees wore a heavy white covering. Beneath them, reds and yellows in the canyon walls caught the morning sun and shone as though with an inner incandescence.

After breakfast we shouldered a light pack, checked camera gear, and headed up the canyon toward Cheyava Falls, full of anticipation.

The temperature had fallen below freezing during the night, even down here, for icicles clung in profusion to trees that overhung the water and received the drift of spray.

We soon arrived at the point where the canyon branched, a larger avenue leading to the right and a lesser to the left.

"Lucky we're not going up that canyon," said the doctor, pointing to the right. "There's no water in it."

We turned up the left fork, obedient to instructions we had received, and followed the little stream, which became smaller as we progressed.

The canyon grew smaller, too, closing in around our heads. All semblance of a trail disappeared—if there had ever been one. The way was often wet. Spring water dripped upon and slickened the rocks where we had to clamber along the bases of the cliffs. Whole ledges lay covered with ice. In coves and overhangs, icicles clung to the walls and roofs, dripping as the sun began to thaw them.

By midday, passage was almost nil. Mesquite and catclaw, leafless but still possessed of their thorns, tore at clothing, hands, and faces. Cactus patches pricked and scraped us. Interlaced thickets of oak barred the way. Vines caught our arms and tangled our feet. It seemed as though we climbed through tropical forest rather than a canyon tributary in an arid land. But the presence of the stream kept us on, and in due course we heard a distant roar.

Everyone stumbled forward helter-skelter, boot heels gouging the

14

Clear Creek: crystal pure and icy cold water in a flood-scarred canyon.

sand, arms flailing to catch a ledge or ward off a limb. If ever a band of explorers felt on the verge of making a great discovery, it was this one.

We came to a slender forty-foot cascade.

"This is Cheyava Falls?" the doctor asked, his face a total blank. "Didn't the Kolb Brothers say that it was a thousand feet high?"

We looked around. The ledge, sheer and without handholds or vegetation, could not be scaled for lack of equipment. We had found an excellent example of a box canyon.

But no Cheyava Falls.

It took all afternoon to get back to camp, through the thickets, across the cactus, along the slippery roads.

"We have one more day," the doctor said that night by the fire. "Shall we lose it also?"

We could only conclude now that the United States Geological Survey was correct, that Cheyava Falls did indeed exist up the right fork rather than the left. But the canyon was dry. . . .

Climbing at dawn among boulders of enormous proportion tumbled and strewn by floods, we found water up that fork the following morning. This, together with the relative openness and easy passage, gave us cause for elation.

Then the stream gave out.

"Dry!" the doctor said.

He sat, dejected, on a boulder. Somewhere up this canyon, he said, was supposed to be a waterfall a thousand feet high.

"Where is the water?" he asked, pointing to the stream bed.

"The Bright Angel shale is porous," we replied.

"So—?"

"The water has gone underground."

He knelt and placed his ear to a rock. "I'll say it has," he said. "About four hundred feet underground!"

By noon we had gone another four miles up the canyon without seeing any more water in the stream bed or, stopping occasionally and letting the silence envelop us, without hearing even the remotest sound of a waterfall.

On a wide sloping rock we ate lunch—cheese and crackers and dried peaches—and at the end of it the doctor announced: "I'm going back."

The others agreed at once, which came as a shock. It had never occurred to us to stop until we had reached the head of the canyon and solved the mystery one way or another.

16

But they would not even consider going "around the next bend." That refrain had become all too familiar.

The doctor said simply, "I fail to see the sense of searching for a thousand-foot waterfall in a bone-dry canyon."

The logic could not be evaded. Time even then was turning against us. The sun had begun to fall toward the blue western rim, and the canyon shadows lengthened.

We appealed again. But it was no use.

As the rest of the party packed up and headed back downstream, we went on, promising to go around one more bend and then, if not successful, catch up and return with them to camp.

That bend proved unfruitful, but we saw at once that around the *next* one would be a more open view up the canyon.

The lure was too much. We broke our promise. It could not be helped.

That bend left still an unobstructed view ahead. Now, however, at the base of a small snow bank a trickle of water soaked the stream bed. Looking ahead we saw that the stream was running again—not much, but it was encouraging.

"Come back! Come back!"

Perhaps the others would hear us and retrace their steps. But our voices only echoed along the cliffs. A subsequent silence was our only answer.

We called again, but the canyon maze swallowed every sound.

We moved on and up—over the boulders and into the sands, into the water—muscles taking on a new resilience. All was forgotten but discovery. Where were the falls?

The Kolbs may have found them forty years before, but that made no difference now. This was a personal discovery.

Time stopped. The world had halted its forward motion. Everything came to a standstill in an unchanging image. The snow on the rim had still not melted. The walls and cliffs remained as red as always. The sound of clambering footsteps seemed magnified, as in an echo chamber.

The last few steps had a dreamlike quality; the kind of dream in which one struggles but makes no progress, hurries but goes too slowly. Or one in which the object sought turns out to be unreal and then nonexistent, and when we reach to grasp it the dream evaporates.

Around a cornice, along an embankment, out of the shade, and up on a pile of boulders. We came to a sudden halt. The scene spread out before and above us, stupendous, unexpected.

Only then, with heart and lungs pumping wildly and head pounding, did the revelation come. Only then, late and inconceivably simple, did we know how a thousand-foot waterfall could exist in a dry canyon.

Cheyava Falls was frozen.

Tons of ice in terrace after terrace glittered in the afternoon sun, solidly white against the sheer face of the Redwall cliff. For an unbroken drop of nearly 500 feet the ice clasped the wall in a dazzling display; then for another 500 the water had frozen by terraced stages over the Bright Angel shale until, step by step, it disappeared, stilled and silent, at the bottom of the canyon.

That so great a phenomenon could be so silent seemed almost impossible. Yet not a sound stirred the vastness. Not a hint of motion or music emerged from this spectacle, nor from anywhere else. No bird, no squirrel, no wind, no crack of ice or fall of rock broke the silence.

We wanted to call out to our friends but it was too late. They were halfway back to camp by now.

The sound faded, and silence returned. The spell of the lonesome canyon, glorious and reassuring, came back.

Our elation was surely no less than Cook's at Van Diemen's Land or Bering's off Kayak Island. They had had no sight like this!

It was a red and white scene, from the snow-encrusted trees on the rim above to the hidden base of the falls. An afternoon haze blurred the south rim, seen through a V-shaped portal of Clear Creek canyon to the south. The west rim of this tributary gorge, almost blocking the sun, rose ponderously in silhouette.

Everything expressed itself on a scale of giantism. Even Cheyava Falls had its place. That which enveloped us consisted of three fundamentals: the canyon, the sky—a deep blue, pure, empty, all-enclosing sky—and the stillness.

18

They seemed to represent a new kind of three-dimensional world, not including time, for time did not exist. And not including distance, for everything was both near and far.

How fragile that spell! The slightest disturbance could have severed the tenuous relation between canyon, sky, and silence.

We could not turn our eyes from the frozen falls: the entire environment had a profound and larger effect, but one catalyzed by the falls.

How many years had gone by without the weather conditions necessary to create such a frozen cascade, we had no idea. We had had the extraordinary fortune—and the persistence, as it happened—to have arrived at the proper moment.

We managed to break our gaze long enough to make some pictures. We wanted to get up to the falls, to examine the ice, to perceive this marvel at close range. But the unmoving cataract lay more than half a mile away, and a sudden chill came over us, literally, as the sun dropped behind the west ridge and left a shadow filled with coolness from the snow above.

Time had not stopped here after all, despite the spell of timelessness. It was midafternoon, with hours of hiking required to reach the camp. Reality came back, and the moment of departure arrived. It was a painful moment. We wanted to stay until the last light faded from the white wall of Cheyava, to absorb strength from the scene and let it flow into our veins as long as it could be discerned. But to go back to camp in darkness, over such rough terrain, even with a flashlight, would have been foolhardy.

With one last look we turned away. It was with quick steps and light heart that we hurried back down the canyon.

As it happened, the doctor and the rest of the party did get to see Cheyava Falls—from nine miles away. We discovered next day, on climbing back out, that the falls could be seen from the south rim of the Canyon.

With binoculars we scanned the distant promontory where sheets of ice still remained, and great terraces of white broke the expanse of red cliff.

The doctor had nothing to say. It was hard to see from the impassivity of his face how he felt about what he beheld. He merely turned and walked on up the trail.

We were about to return to the world of rules, where we would have to watch ourselves and do acceptable things. But with or without Cheyava Falls we could tell that the doctor was different from the time a few days ago when we had broken away from the rim, and from society, and started down the trail. He had not seen at close hand what he went to see, but had perhaps found something more valuable.

The spell had caught up with him, as it had with us. We would never be quite the same again.

2

ANIMAL TRACKS

A FEW MONTHS later we returned to the south-rim forest. The snow was gone. The grass was green and rich.

We had not seen the doctor again, or the other members of the party. They had gone their separate, busy ways and we ours. But we had never been so busy that we did not yearn to breathe again that fragrant air, to enter for a while the deepest part of the woods, to discover the hidden habits of the deer, the dove, the squirrel.

Summer rain had washed the air. A scent of pine and sagebrush permeated the open forest and spilled over yellowish cliffs into the meadows below. Fernbush filled the mountain air with an almost purifying sweetness. Its flowers called to every winged insect within range.

Whether any of these scents appealed to the tassel-eared squirrel, or were even noticed by it, we had no way of knowing. Nothing in the squirrel's behavior said so. Like other life in this semiarid forest, the squirrel responded vigorously to the end of a summer shower. A rebirth, almost a reburst, of action came as the heat of the sun melted the chill of rain and warmed the clean air.

We had always found that the time just after a rain was best for observations in this upland forest. Now, on a day in July, 1948, we had come upon an Abert squirrel and thought we might follow it to see where it went and what it did.

This was about six months after the trip to Cheyava Falls. We had both been appointed ranger-naturalists at Grand Canyon National Park, with duties almost as widely varied as nature itself. To deal

Ponderosa needles and cones begin the soil-enriching process of decay.

with the geology of the Canyon in public talks, to lead forest walks, to present campfire programs, and above all to field a thousand questions a day, required a diligent pursuit of knowledge about nature in and around the Canyon.

The mammals most commonly seen in forests through which visitors had to approach Grand Canyon were mule deer and Abert squirrels. There were thus frequent queries about those species, the squirrel being least known and perhaps most intriguing to newcomers.

Each ranger-naturalist spent hours in the wild domain to prepare himself for the daily deluge of questions. And he was fully aware that he had to understand each animal not by its deeds alone but by the company it kept and the world in which it lived.

Rain had changed nearly everything, and the animal hurried along as though it had only a day to remain in the universe. Elegance marked its moves. Haste hardly interfered with grace as it leaped and paused, leaped and paused. Like the rolling surface of a gentle wave, the squirrel arched its back and followed through with an upward-downward sweep of the flaring tail.

It stopped. Not the slightest movement, not a flicker of a whisker, not a twitching of eye could be seen. The red fur glowed as sunlight streamed on it, and the bold gray-white tail poised as a wave poises before breaking into spray. The large ears, normally tasseled, lacked their pointed tufts at this season.

We were not privileged to know why the squirrel stopped, or why it moved on. It had not given the slightest indication as to where it was going. What turned it right and what turned it left were universal laws of guidance quite unapparent to us. One thing was obvious, however: the squirrel seemed absolutely at home, an integral part of the forest.

Open, parklike, airy, free—this ponderosa-pine community might have been anywhere in the American West. The tall and stately boles, orange-plated and free of stubs or branches for much of their height, gave the pine a massive command over its environment.

But this was not just any part of the American West. It was part of the world's largest forest of ponderosa pine, and here it had become anchored virtually in solid rock, seeking whatever soil had been manufactured from the Kaibab limestone, which wasn't much.

The seemingly solid surface of the rock was rent with tiny cracks and solution crevices in which the barest hint of soil had begun to form. Despite the scarcity of rainfall, plants thrived in an infinite array of forms and colors: the green and bluish gray of moss; the chartreuse, orange, gray, black, and blue of lichens; the star-shaped forms, the dendritic, the rounded amorphous masses, the radiating patterns where nodules or fossils had weathered out.

We found these things so changeable and compelling that we soon lost track of the squirrel.

After the rain, every pocket that could possibly hold a little water did so, mirroring the sky in nearly every surface, as though a thousand crystals of quartz had been embedded and faceted on the exterior of the rocks. The limestone was as bright as it ever gets, and the new-washed needles of pine appeared more green than ever. Twisted trunks of juniper, endowed with curls and scrolls, seemed to have been washed and polished in the same way that a piece of sculpture is cleaned and placed on exhibition.

The squirrel's primary, but not exclusive, interest lies in ponderosa pines. It can and does have some variation in diet, but its main food supply is the inner bark of twig ends, which it clips several inches behind the terminal bud and strips to get at the juices and flesh within.

This is the fundamental year-round food, although pine seeds are probably more palatable and more desirable when available. So well does this squirrel fit into the ponderosa world that it readily singles out the best-tasting trees and clips them vigorously, just as an eastern squirrel singles out a special elm and almost defoliates it in spring.

One squirrel may clip nearly a hundred twigs in a day, chew them a while and drop them to the ground. Few other animals, notably porcupines and certain insects, even come close to competing for this kind of food, so the squirrel's life appears at first to be idyllic.

Yet water is sometimes unavailable to the tree in sufficient quantity for production of seeds or good bark tissue, and the squirrel may know famine. Populations of the squirrel are known to fluctuate from one year to another.

In any case, the tassel-eared squirrel is trapped. A progression of time and life has tied it to this forest and this tree. It cannot even visit its neighbor cousins which have been isolated perhaps through the removal of once-contiguous forests. Now the intervening expanses devoid of ponderosa pines constitute a biological barrier to travel.

The tassel-ear also affects ponderosa forests, for when squirrel population is high, most seeds are dug out and eaten rather than allowed to fall, germinate, and sprout.

23

There is nothing "unnatural" about this, and little cause for alarm. This kind of activity has been going on for perhaps thousands of centuries. Tree and squirrel lived in harmony long before man came, and their relation became perfected to a careful point of balance. That balance wavered from time to time, responsive to good years or bad, but balance it was, and is, and neither pines nor squirrels—nor their environment—seem to suffer permanently from fluctuations in weather or nutrient supply.

Such harmony, almost flawless, is difficult for man to emulate. He worries about the balance because he himself alters it without knowing fully how or how seriously. Actually, the grand alliance of squirrel and pine is a product of change itself. When the seed crop is abundant and the squirrels are not, whole forests of ponderosa take root and begin to grow.

We are thus left with the conclusion that the squirrel does not seriously affect the reproductive capacity of the pines.

It is probably quite ignorant of its place in this society, where its old nests benefit porcupines, which use them as resting platforms, and chipmunks, which use them as places to raise their young, and where jackrabbits feed on the clipped twig-ends beneath the pines. If such clippings fall on top of a heavy snow, rabbits may find them mightily welcome.

We soon caught up with the squirrel, determined now to pursue it as far as we could, gathering what facts we might in regard to its behavior and relation to surroundings. There was an enduring, almost urgent need for this kind of data, the science of ethology (animal behavior) being yet in infancy and ecology rising rapidly. As naturalists interpreting to the public almost daily a synthesis of the squirrel's world, we had to know it as best we could.

The challenge was not without disadvantages. We had to observe the world of the squirrel and the pine through eyes not trained to see as the squirrel saw. We had to deduce from insights founded on human rather than rodential training. And as much as possible, we had to beware of human approaches to rodential processes.

No matter for the moment. We had our quarry in sight again.

The tassel-ear seemed not to notice the abundance of food or water available. It passed by seed cones, ignored fungi and acorns, and paid no attention to discarded bones that it may have chewed on at one time or another. It paid no attention (that we saw) to the fresh supplies of water on the rocks, perhaps because it usually gets a supply of moisture from food or manufactures a small amount metabolically as other rodents do.

Something else seemed on its mind. Danger perhaps, which is always present, day and night. The squirrel has been equipped for danger by awareness, ability to dash and dodge, a reliance on lack of motion when necessary, or by the blending color of its pelage. Still, the swoop of a hawk or an owl or an eagle, the pounce of a fox or coyote, the stealthy approach of a bobcat or mountain lion, or the strike of a rattlesnake are to be watched for, perhaps even planned for. The squirrel's ancestors had evolved quick warning and reaction systems, though not all ambushes could be avoided.

It was a beautiful day! The clouds had gone. The sky, as it generally did in Arizona, became a rich, incomparable blue—the blue of a deep volcanic lake. The scent of freshness and the presence of lingering mists above each shadowed vale gave a whole new zest to the forest. We, too, lingered to absorb it momentarily, lest it escape and be lost, and then went on.

Suddenly, the spell was broken by the sound of speeding automobiles on a road that had been cut through the forest. The squirrel paid little heed, approaching the pavement without a change of pace.

The age-old warning system in its brain had failed to function. Nothing had prepared it for this kind of enemy.

In the middle of the road some inner intuition told it to stop. The automobile sped toward it like a bullet. There was no instinctive evolutionary action. The squirrel became confused at this attack. It knew not which way to rush, for this giant metallic creature did not fly as a hawk does, or leap like a coyote, or strike in the manner of a rattlesnake. It just kept roaring and coming on.

At the final possible moment the squirrel dug its claws into the pavement and flattened its body for maximum speed, getting away with only milliseconds to spare.

The car zoomed off but left behind a trail of unfamiliar odors that spread for a short way into the woods.

At a reassuring distance from the road and the odors, the tassel-ear felt more at ease. A chattering chickadee made no obvious ripple in the squirrel's demeanor. The two lived parallel lives that seldom or never conflicted.

The squirrel soon found itself in surroundings that differed from its native haunts of ponderosa pine. Gradually, more specimens of juniper and pinyon pine mixed in, and the stately ponderosa diminished in numbers. The forest trees became much smaller in stature, more twisted and less stately, the trunks of pinyon black, not orange.

But the pinyon bore seeds, important food to a squirrel. And the juniper wore a shaggy bark without which the squirrel's nest might not have as soft a lining. The mating season had been some weeks ago, perhaps scarcely remembered now with the sexual organs retracted, the urge abated, the body chemistry subdued, the birth accomplished, and the young in charge of their mother.

The squirrel broke into a run again, alert for spines of cactus hidden in snakeweed as if to spear the passerby, and alert for bayonet-like leaves of yucca, which clustered around the base of a pinyon tree or menaced from amid the grass.

On the rare patches of barren soil we knelt to examine the squirrel's tracks, mingled with those of other animals that shared its domain. Shrews and skunks it seldom saw, owing to their nocturnal habits, but rock squirrels, chipmunks, mice, rats, rabbits, mule deer, and birds were plentiful, and equally part of the rim community.

The squirrel moved on into an almost pure forest of pinyon pines, some stately, some small, some leaning against others, some twisted, their cones of earlier years flung across the forest floor.

With the right kind of shadows the trees could have been a ballet of witches, their forms whirling wildly, awkwardly posed, leaning over, or fallen to the ground and clutching it in a variety of ways. Downed tree trunks had become homes for insects and were decaying, a slow process where only sixteen inches of rain fall a year.

Some trees had been decaying so long that they were turning into an enriching dust that added organic matter to the soil. This dust spurred the growth of new generations of plants, which in turn spurred the growth of squirrels and mice and rabbits.

And that in turn spurred the growth of larger animals that fed on them. Pascal had been right; the French philosopher recognized in his *Pensées* that nature was set in a balance. The great philosopher-naturalist, John Muir, put it another way: everything in this universe, he said, is hitched to everything else.

26

A cable was next on the tassel-ear's itinerary. A rusted cable, strung from one tree to another, had fallen to the ground and lain there frayed and broken for half a century or more. There were also bits of glass and rusted metal, old tin cans, twisted pipes, and other debris of a different epoch.

Evening shadows at the rim, the Colorado River below.

Jumping over the cable and making its way along pathways through the grass, the squirrel followed a route of its own—unpaved, unsigned, but apparently familiar. The sudden screech of a Steller's jay, unnerving and startling to man, caused scarcely a swerve in the animal's forward movement. Its nerves, set tautly for other things, were scarcely strummed by jays, or by the songs of robins. Those nerves were tuned to the scream of the hawk.

Again the squirrel stopped, this time on a rock, head up, ears high. We wondered about the missing tassels and what function the ear tufts served, if not to attract a mate. They are shed in summer months, and regrown in autumn as though having something to do with the change of pelage.

This pelage is about as varied as that on any mammal in North America: grizzly gray on most of the body, a rusty band along the back, a thin black line at the sides, white fur on the stomach and undersides of the tail, and gray fur on the upper portion of the tail.

The tassel-ear seemed in a hurry, but we could hardly imagine it to have any more than a vague concept of time. As Aldo Leopold said, time, to an atom locked in a rock, does not pass.

At that moment, time seemed only a minor tool occasionally used by men. The squirrel concerned itself with more important things, like nuts and twigs and hawks.

These occupied it more than its relation to the pine, or the pine's relation to sagebrush, or sagebrush to soil, or soil to pine, and pine to squirrel again. That circle meant less than the circle of seasons. To know the spring by mating call, the summer by waves of heat, the autumn by frosty nights, and the winter by heavy snows was to know the essentials of the year.

Aside from sensitivity to the seasons, the Abert has a few other things in common with men: origin, a little physiology, capacity to reproduce. But there the connection ends. The squirrel has lived and thrived and flourished in this forest for thousands of years, without any improvements or protection by man. It has, in an extraordinarily complex way, evolved right along with the rest of the rim community.

28

The squirrel seemed not to notice the great canyon to which it came at last. Its only natural duty was to keep from falling over the rim, a task no tougher than avoiding a fall from a tree.

At the edge of the white limestone escarpment that marked the end of land and beginning of space, the animal paused.

An old dead pinyon tree, gripped by solid rock, bent over the rim.

How many seasons it must have endured, unsheltered at the brink, no one could tell. Its needles, brown and crisp, still clutched the limbs, and the limbs still reached for open sky as though to soak up energy for a resumption of life.

But life would not resume there; all around grew other, newer pinyons, heavily needled, bursting with cones, filled with seeds to be harvested and stored or clipped and eaten by the inhabitants of the forest. Life renews itself abundantly in these woods. Signs of growth and birth lie everywhere.

Now came a playful twitch of the broad gray tail. Over a field of scattered, angular boulders, into and out of a mountain-mahogany clump, past a twisted patriarchal sagebrush that looked as though it had been growing on this rim for centuries, over a ridge and down a cliff the Abert leaped with what human beings might interpret as little less than the joy of life.

Once over the cliff, where tassel-ears rarely go, it entered a forest containing Douglas fir and other plants that thrived in cool locations. The elevation dropped away rapidly and foods familiar to rim-dwelling squirrels became scarce. Ponderosa pines did not succeed very well in this environment. Juniper and pinyon obviously grew less abundantly, too. Without them, the squirrel could not proceed much lower.

Its curiosity apparently satisfied, it turned away, unmindful of the gorge, the haze, the bright red walls, the distant river, the swirling swallows and swifts. Its eyes, through centuries of animal tradition, have come to focus on other things.

Its below-rim venture ended, the Abert turned and scampered up the slopes and cliffs, over the edge of the rim, back under the yucca and through a patch of fern bush into the pinyon-juniper forest.

Minutes later, or an hour later, it was back among the ponderosa pines. A quiet, timeless voice had signaled that this was where it belonged.

3

SOUTH RIM

When not searching out the secrets of individual animals, we engaged in efforts to understand interactions between plants and animals and the relation of all living things to the rocks and soil on which they grew.

Precious little was known about such things in the 1940's—precious little is now—but naturalists on the staff saw with their own eyes something of what was going on in the wild, and from their experiences drew raw material for public programs.

Wanting ways to show how everything is woven into the web of life, we attempted to obtain photographs that would make unmistakably clear what eats what in the natural flow of living energy. The south-rim forest provided nearly all that was needed in this regard, and the inner canyon added starkly different dimensions.

But one day, almost by accident, we happened on something that touched public sensitivity more than anything else.

We knew that most human beings came to the Grand Canyon for one basic reason; to get a look at the great gorge they had heard so much about.

Over and over we watched them walk to the rim and look in for the first time, and something seemed to change inside them, rivet them to the spot and silence them. There were those whose breath was literally taken away, who returned from the edge of the precipice with their eyes working strangely, and obviously some kind of a lump in their throats.

"Good God!" they would say, if they said anything at all, or "My Heavens!" or "Will you look at that!" in a very low voice. Some just shook their heads. Some sat on a bench or leaned on a railing and were quiet for a long time, as though trying to reorganize confused and chaotic thoughts.

Some shook with fear, and clutched a railing or a tree and made their way back from the edge to sit down and quiet their pounding hearts.

A few didn't seem much affected. One man took a look and then came over and said: "You ought to do something with all that open wasteland between Williams and here. Sixty miles! We wouldn't let that kind of land go to waste in New Jersey. We'd *do* something with it."

Every fifth person, it seemed, repeated the old saws about the Canyon being a good place to throw razor blades or lose a cow. Others had heard the story about a cheapskate having dug this hole while looking for a lost nickel, or the tale of that old pioneer guide and sometime hotelkeeper John Hance, who claimed to have dug the Canyon and hauled the dirt away to build up San Francisco Peaks, near Flagstaff.

Another oldtimer said that he had seen women faint at the sight of it and strong men weep over it, but not one who expected it. An old wrangler reckoned that Zion Canyon, about eighty-five miles north in Utah, was man's size and the Grand Canyon God's size.

The Canyon, 217 miles long, four to eighteen miles wide, and a mile deep, was always, it seemed to us, a little hard for the human mind to grasp. It was of little consequence that other valleys might be deeper, wider, or more colorful; this one was most spectacular, most striking, most mysterious.

In some ways, the scene was hard to grasp because it was hard to measure—there was nothing with which to compare this Canyon.

"It is not to be comprehended in a day or a week, nor even in a month," said the pioneer geologist, Clarence E. Dutton. "It must be dwelt upon and studied, and the study must comprise the slow acquisitions of the meaning and spirit of that marvelous scenery which characterizes the Plateau Country, and of which the great chasm is the superlative manifestation."

31

Not everyone, of course, was willing to wait for a slow acquisition of knowledge, or to acquire much knowledge at all. Mules were available to carry a man limply into and out of the gorge; air flights could sweep him down beside ridges and deep among the black rocks of the bottom. If that palled, he could spend hours in curio shops, examining merchandise also on sale in a thousand stores throughout the Southwest, or sit in a cocktail lounge with other human beings from all parts of the world and talk to them endlessly—while a world full of miracles awaited unseen outside.

Still, the majority behaved as though this natural phenomenon, however mystifying, was the greatest show on earth, and we saw a good many people abandon the temptations of shops and bars and lounges, and go out on the rim pathways to be by themselves and discover things that they had never seen or felt before, things not on sale anywhere.

This was the key that should have unlocked the secret of our later discovery, but at the time we did not quite realize the intensity of feeling the Canyon engenders.

"These are the footprints of Creation," said John C. Van Dyke, the author and philosopher, more than half a century ago, "beside which those of the human seem so small and so inconsequential. Why was association with the work of man ever invoked here at the Canyon? Nothing that he ever did looks other than foolish compared with the master-work of Nature."

That view may seem a bit extreme now, but there are many who adopt it. Others find the framework fashioned by John Wesley Powell, the nineteenth-century explorer and geologist, more revealing of perspective:

Every one of these almost innumerable gorges is a world of beauty in itself. In the Grand Canyon there are thousands of gorges like that below Niagara Falls, and there are a thousand Yosemites. Yet all these canyons unite to form one grand canyon, the most sublime spectacle on the earth. Pluck up Mt. Washington by the roots to the level of the sea and drop it headfirst into the Grand Canyon, and the dam will not force its waters over the walls. Pluck up the Blue Ridge and hurl it into the Grand Canyon, and it will not fill it.

Views from the rim support the testimony of poets, and there is little question about the Canyon's being huge and spectacular. Nevertheless, the average visitor sometimes finds the views a bit repetitious, for he is not accustomed to so much color, so much openness, so complicated an earth structure. Not being a geologist he is unable to trace the clues in the cliffs that reveal extraordinary happenings in the past. Not being a botanist he may fail to recognize the significance of changing life patterns from rim to river.

The view from Hopi Point may seem to him the sheerest and most awe-inspiring but he finds it difficult to differentiate that view from

" . . . a world of beauty in itself."

the one at Grandview Point. They are, after all, from the same rim of the same canyon. At one point or another he gets a glimpse of the Colorado River, a close-up of a trail, or a breathtaking look into a yawning abyss that drops away almost sheer at his feet.

But to a certain degree these visions coalesce into an ensemble, and even though it is viewed from many sides it is still the same ensemble. And since it is patently incomprehensible to the newcomer, perhaps for the full length of his first visit and for several visits thereafter, he is likely to want literally to escape into the woods.

This was another key we should have recognized.

"I much prefer Zion Canyon," a visitor once said. "You are down in it. You can get closer to it."

"Well," said another, "this place is all right, but Oak Creek Canyon —there's a real nice canyon that has a creek and some trees."

The words came almost in tones of relief: a creek and some trees. Something familiar, something measurable.

And so at the Grand Canyon the minds of the perceptive turned graspingly toward something they could readily recognize, something within their own range of perception and understanding.

As a visitor approaches the Grand Canyon from any direction, he must come uphill to reach the rim, a slow and gradual ascent that lifts him, at the south rim, to an elevation of over seven thousand feet above sea level. In so rising, he sees the grasslands change to sagebrush flats, the sagebrush mix with straggling junipers, and finally a coalition of juniper, pinyon, and ponderosa pine.

Life would not at first seem easy here, and in places the forest is open and the flora scantily spread. In other places, by contradiction, the vegetation is so thick that you can scarcely see a hundred yards through the woods.

Adaptation to extremes looks very much like the answer, for whatever inhabits this land must endure occasional subzero cold of winter as well as the wind-driven desiccation of spring. Each plant must be constitutionally able to withstand April, May, and June, whose combined precipitation is scarcely an inch.

34

Perhaps it is partly because of mutual-assistance programs that this rim community has thrived so well for so many centuries. The pinyon jay eats pinyon nuts and juniper berries, carrying the seeds away and dropping them in distant places, thus helping in the dispersal of plants.

The yucca, a member of the lily family, depends on the unique pollinating capabilities of the yucca moth. Since only that insect pollinates the yucca, and in turn derives its own food from the plant, we can well imagine how the one life form depends on the other, and what would happen to one if the other suffered damage or elimination. Fragile is the word for that affair.

This forest is filled with action morning, noon, or night. Some times of day are less active than others as far as the wildlife is concerned, and early morning seems to be when birds and mammals are most busy. But we can discern fresh wonders at almost any time and any place, some of them delicate and fleeting.

We may follow the spring of a fawn mule deer as it speeds off through the forest to rejoin its mother. A butterfly settles on the magenta blossom of a thistle; its wings of brown, gold, black, and white seem to have a structure as complex as that of the flower.

One day we found a Utah agave, or century plant, whose flowering stalk had just begun to expand. The time was early June. The sky hung blue and cloudless over the canyon, and we wondered how anything could grow. Summer heat was about to reach its maximum intensity, and the annual spring drought seemed almost at its peak. Heat waves blurred the sharp outlines along the rim and the tops of temples appeared to quiver.

Despite extremes of drought and temperature, agaves flourish on the canyon rim and across inner slopes or terraces. For twenty years or so each remains unspectacular, a discreet rosette of gray, succulent, sharp-pointed leaves. Then one day a scape, or flower-bearing stem, begins to rise. At that point a natural engine of growth goes to work, and the plant expends its entire life energy in pushing up an enormous stalk.

We were curious to see how fast this stalk came up. Rapid growth, we knew, was characteristic of tropical forest plants where fifteen feet of rain fell every year. But here the plants receive little more than fifteen inches a year, and summer rains rarely come until July. It seemed incongruous that the plant would grow at all, much less produce so great a mass in so short a time.

Beside the burgeoning stalk we planted a slender stake on which to record the progress of the growing point. At first we recorded only two or three inches a day. But when the stalk reached four feet high, the stretch-out increased dramatically. Four inches a day, then five, six, seven, eight, nine, ten.

Finally the stalk towered ten feet above our heads, its abundant yellow flowers open to the insects of the rim. The upper portion then departed from the discipline of erectness with which growth

35

had begun. Lacking the built-in strength of the lower stem, it curled and twisted to one side. After that it began to weaken and die, responding to breezes that played along the Canyon rim.

On plateaus below, the stalks of agave exhibit grotesquely distorted flowering stems. Often on steep terraces they bend outward and upward as though striving to free themselves and soar into the void.

Elsewhere they cling to the white limestone of the rim, just out of reach across narrow gulfs that drop 3,000 feet, protected from the trampling feet and prying fingers of men. The bright yellow flowers against the sky, or against the red rock of the inner cliffs, help make the rapidly growing agave one of the regal presences in this rim forest.

Of similar status is cliff rose, a flowering shrub that may reach considerable heights—up to twenty-five feet—and possess a handsome, twisted trunk with shaggy bark.

The flowers open up in a gentle yellow, with petals so persistent that some endure well into October. What one remembers most, however, is the fragrance bestowed by this shrub upon the forest, which already possesses an elegant aroma of sagebrush and juniper and pinyon.

So pervasive is the sweetness of cliff rose that every shadow seems redolent of it, every air endowed with it. One almost becomes mesmerized in its spell; of all the fragrances imprinted upon man's centers of memory, that of cliff rose is one most likely to endure.

The insects appear to agree. Cliff rose is steadily surrounded by a cloud of flying forms. In early summer, when life slows down for want of rain, the shrub attracts a host of insects. So does fernbush, another favorite of arid regions. Both belong to the rose family, but fernbush leaves have deeper dissections, giving the impression of tiny ferns with their multiple pinnae. These leaves are aromatic, which reinforces the fragrance of the white and yellow flowers.

36 Despite extremes of heat and cold and desiccating drought, the fernbush still thrusts its handsome flowers forth for the work of reproduction. The shrub gets along in the barest soil, or what appears to be no soil at all, growing from cracks in the otherwise solid limestone.

At the very edge of the canyon, occasionally even over the brink, we watch the feathery seed tufts of Apache plume perform a deli-

Hopi Point: seed tufts of Apache plume.

cate dance in the wind. A pincushion cactus perches on the rocky rim, giving its glorious colors to attract the insects. The yellow-flowered snakeweed infiltrates nearly every crevice, every patch of soil, every terrace. Locoweed leaves a lavender trail. Red and yellow Gaillardias, swaying like sunflowers, speckle the slopes. Almost sulphurlike in yellow intensity, flowering buckwheat seeks open, sun-baked flats. Phlox chooses rocks. Paperflowers unfold their yellow clusters on dry embankments. Fleabanes gather in gravels.

One after another, the south-rim roll call of plants reveals a highly diversified natural garden. Goldenrod. Aster. Lupine. Rabbit brush. Milkweed. Wallflower. Lotus. And scores of others.

The twisted plumes of cliff rose as well as mountain mahogany demonstrate the manner in which some plants have specialized in an arid land: these spiral awns twist and untwist with changes in moisture, so that when the ground becomes wet and soft they curl and drive their seed heads into the soil. This self-sowing process, produced by the genetics of centuries, helps these plants to thrive where others would perish. Certain other seeds also have this sharp-pointed base and corkscrewlike tail, apparently for identical reasons. Thus our roving senses discern not only fragrant flowers but miracles of evolution and persistence of life as well.

If the south-rim forest is fragrant and colorful, it is also serene. At times it is filled with music.

You can walk among the pinyon trees when neither sound nor movement disturbs the scene, when only a mystic quiet prevails. But such times do not last long. The forest comes to life with wild music, different music, light, profound, symphonic, melodious, varied. Well known are the tones strummed by breezes in the trees. Naturalists say that the sound of wind through a pinyon differs from the sigh of wind through needles of ponderosa. They can almost distinguish the difference with their eyes closed. This seems only proper, for the needles of ponderosa are sometimes a foot in length, whereas those of pinyon grow less than two inches in length and are often curved.

Each tree constitutes a different instrument. Each has different high-pitched notes. Even the bass differs. Ponderosas seem full throated, as though the wind were echoing in a hollow amphitheater. Pinyons remain higher strung, more intimate. And being less lordly, they give us a feeling of cheerfulness rather than awe.

This intimacy with nature, with things simple—the relief from sights overwhelming—all contributed to our discovery of the other side of the Grand Canyon: its silence and simple life.

The mention of these things before public audiences aroused more interest, awe and comment than we expected at first—as though we had touched upon something each person deeply felt but had never dared to hope was shared by others.

Then came the day we made our confirming discovery. In passing a clump of Gambel oak we stopped suddenly, eyes caught by a special sparkle of green. We had seen this oak a thousand times (it is very common), seen the sun glint on it, reveled in the richness of its green against the sky.

But now the sunlight streamed through this one leaf in a way that we had never noticed before. The leaf was not unlike other oak leaves, yet on that morning, the sun had caught it at a perfect moment, as a spotlight catches an emerald on exhibition. It stood out among all the other leaves in sight.

Light passed through the translucent green blade, making it seem to glow with inner radiant energy. It seemed absurd at first to be so struck with the color of a leaf here, of all places, on the rim of a great canyon that possesses color and form and spectacle in every conceivable combination. It is easy to ask, at such times, how a simple sunlit leaf could compare with so immense a wonder just a few steps away.

But this green blade of living protoplasm and that great gorge of stone were fashioned by the same forces, under related principles and natural laws. The veins running through the leaf, intricately and finely formed, required in their manufacture as complicated a mechanism as does the making of rock strata, or the manufacture of squirrels. That demonstrated a certain oneness about this world, too real to dismiss, yet too all-encompassing to embrace with ease.

We took a picture of the leaf, and the resulting transparency, more than any other illustration, captured the imagination of audiences wherever we spoke. From the enthusiastic responses we received at the Grand Canyon, and later elsewhere in the United States and around the world, it became abundantly clear that the human mind is as receptive to the small, simple, fragile beauty in nature as to the massiveness and glory of enormous geologic wonders.

You do not forget the little things of the forest—the leaf in sunlight, the trusting pygmy nuthatch that flew to your hand unafraid and ate some seeds you offered, the white-breasted nuthatch that scarcely stirred even though you sat beside the tree trunk within arm's reach of it.

We cared for newborn chipmunks so tiny they had to be fed

with milk from an eyedropper. We watched as twin fawns browsed with their mother, aware of us but largely unconcerned.

Such miracles are not possible in every forest, because not every forest has been kept so free from the disturbances of man.

At dusk we listened to the rasp of a nighthawk, and stopped in the silence awaiting the musical, humming whir of wings as it pulled out of a long, steep dive, all part of the mating process.

The evolution of centuries has been at work on this south-rim forest. The changes of millenniums have fitted every plant and animal into its surroundings.

The trees bestow juices to appease the hunger of sapsuckers. They offer raw material for the nests of squirrels, wood rats, and birds. In turn these animals help to spread the seeds of trees, and thus all species increase and prosper and disperse.

Man cannot yet re-create conditions conducive to such evolution, or the evolutionary act itself. He has made attempts to restore some animal forms by breeding back but habitat damage is painful to species whose delicate balance with their environment is disturbed. We cannot always repair what we ruin. We do not know how. And extinction is terribly final.

In the south-rim forest an endless succession of life upon life goes on, most of it unseen by man. It is not his milieu. He is seldom willing or possessed of sufficient patience to watch the tassel-eared squirrel leave its nest at sunrise, feed intensively for hours, rest, travel, climb, clean itself, leap among the trees, dig in the litter for seeds and feed intermittently until sundown, then return to its high-perched nest.

And if we therefore do not know exactly how the life of the moth relates to that of the lizard, the swallow, the skunk, wood rat, vole, porcupine, fox, and bobcat, then we need to be cautious in "caring" for these animals and the forest in which they live. Wildlife owes allegiance not to man but to natural laws, the complexity of which we are finally beginning to discover.

For more than fifty years this forest has been part of a national park wherein the Congressional mandate has been "to conserve the scenery and the natural and historic objects and the wildlife therein and to provide for the enjoyment of the same in such manner and by such means as will leave them unimpaired for the enjoyment of future generations."

How much longer it will be possible to do all that is the question of the day. Until now, the rim forest has been reasonably well protected, and as far as we know, most of its original complex ecological relationships are still intact. This is thus a near-virgin area where research under natural conditions can be conducted. But human beings are influencing the environment—without knowing the effect on these delicately balanced networks of life.

The wilderness of the Grand Canyon may be in more trouble than we think.

4

INDIAN COUNTRY

TIME HAS FORGOTTEN the names of those who first discovered the Grand Canyon—if they had any names. No written records remain of that discovery so we can pay homage to no single individual. The first men must have left little more than footprints.

As hunters or gatherers, these men probably took back to their desert homes whatever minerals, hides, or other natural products abounded in this region. Perhaps they came into pinyon country seeking seeds at a time of harvest.

The earliest records are scant and obscure, except that in places several hundred miles away projectile points have been found associated with mammals that since became extinct.

With the progression of millenniums, more hunters and gatherers settled in the Southwest. They learned the cultivation of corn at least two thousand years before Christ, added beans and squash to their home-grown menu, and in due time found themselves relying on agriculture more than on hunting.

Thus began human culture, of Asiatic origin, in the desert and canyon country. With more time to think than had originally been required for hunting and gathering and self-defense, the people developed clothing, ornamentation, basketry, and housing that became increasingly sophisticated.

From simple pit houses they advanced to communal Pueblo buildings with three hundred rooms. From little or no clothing, they succeeded to elaborate sandals, blankets, and robes, and then to colorfully woven textiles.

Echo Cliffs and Marble Canyon, north of the Grand Canyon.

By A.D. 1000 these communities had sprung up in what is now the Four Corners region, where Utah, Arizona, Colorado, and New Mexico meet. The people constructed thousands of Pueblo villages. Apartment-like dwellings proliferated, some on canyon ledges, some in caves, some at the edges of streams. Trade among tribes grew rapidly and flourished.

But then, for several reasons, this burgeoning artistic civilization began to disintegrate. People grew restless. Crops failed during periods of drought. Strife must have developed, as it so often does with the increase and confinement of organisms.

Centers of population sprang up and declined at the Grand Canyon too. Man-made objects discovered within the Canyon have been dated as far back as three thousand years. But it was apparently not until A.D. 600 or 700 that Basketmakers occupied the north rim and Cohonina Indians the south rim.

A few pueblos, containing up to thirty rooms, were in time built on the rims. Altogether, nearly a thousand sites have been identified in and near the Canyon, but probably only a few were occupied at any one time. The Canyon never had a highly developed population such as those at Mesa Verde, Chaco Canyon, and Kayenta in the San Juan River country.

Between A.D. 1185 and 1200 the Pueblo people constructed a village now called Tusayan, set in the pinyon-juniper forest of the south rim. Perhaps thirty occupants lived in this U-shaped, stone-walled, two-story structure, but not for very long.

A time of drought had come, and by the end of the thirteenth century this and many another Pueblo village lay empty, silent, and slowly beginning to crumble.

Where all the people went is not precisely known, but by the time the first Europeans arrived—Spanish explorers from Mexico—the Pueblo Indians had concentrated in groups such as the Hopi and Zuñi, living not so much in cliffs, as before, but on the tops of mesas. So ended an era.

44 But not an ideology.

There could hardly have been a greater clash of ideas, of principles, of beliefs, of goals than that between the Indians and the Spanish.

The Hopi, for example, had become extremely well adapted to a land that, because of its aridity, produces something less than full biological potential. What it did produce they made splendid use of. What it lacked they somehow made up for.

Prudently, they used it all. Currants and cactus fruits they ate outright, and many leafy plants they cooked for greens. Tools they made from oak and other hardwoods, dyes from saltbush, and many kinds of medicines from plants: sagebrush for digestive disorders; paintbrush to prevent conception. Yucca was soap, laxative, and textile fiber. Cotton they knew and raised. Corn grew under their watchful eyes and careful tending, corn in purple, yellow, white, blue, red, and multicolored ears. They turned the ubiquitous juniper into firewood, food, construction material, and medicine.

They had cosmetics and chewing gum. And a beneficent universe saw to it that they had all sorts of ceremonial material with which to carry out the purposes of their rituals, their dances, their meditations.

The Hopis possessed a complex religious ceremonialism with a fundamentally simple design: to maintain the harmony of the universe. *Hopi* itself means "peace." The concept of peace was at the core of the souls, the actions, and the hopes of these people.

"They remind us," wrote Frank Waters in his *Book of the Hopi* that "we must attune ourselves to the need for inner change if we are to avert a cataclysmic rupture between our own minds and hearts. Now, if ever, is the time for them to talk, for us to listen."

It is not easy, of course, to listen and more difficult to understand, especially for persons who have been taught to think that man was created to stand apart from nature. The Hopis believe that all parts of the universe are interrelated, which would mean that man is a part of rather than apart from the universe.

Hopi myths quite clearly specify that there are things to be learned from animals: industry, planning, and self-reliance, for example. The eagle (a national emblem of both Mexico and the United States) is revered by them. The Parrot Clan is the symbolic mother of Hopi clans, second only to the Bear Clan in importance. These two, plus the Badger and Eagle, are the four most important clans. Others are named after coyotes, spiders, bluebirds, crows, butterflies, rabbits, fog, sand, cloud, and so on.

To Hopis, beauty dwells in the simplest of things. The healing 45 power of music figures in their religion. Sunflowers, as far as they are concerned, are simply flower maidens imbued with life from identical sources (sun and soil and water) as we. The skunk symbolizes the sun because its scent reaches out like solar rays, which grant the gift of life to living things. Spruce is a sacred tree, and turquoise a stone that embodies the spiritual qualities of water, sky, and plant life.

The Hopi priests (though they have no formal priesthood) prayed for unity and harmony among all forms of life, an ecological thesis that may well antedate scientific discovery of the principles of inter-related plant and animal communities. The Hopis saw man not as a conqueror of the earth but simply enmeshed with all living things, not a master of mountains and seas and the stars, but a neighbor of them, unwise to act independently. Man had his place, they implied, and it was strictly limited.

Beauty, harmony, nature, the reverence of natural objects rather than sanctified men . . . the arriving Spaniards must have thought these strange bases for construction of a religion. The Spaniards walked a different path—to glory, to power, to wealth, to conquest and conversion of other human beings, to a world in which man was everything, fashioned even in the image of one god.

The Hopis seemed a simple people, lacking guns, horses, and books, having not even the vestige of a wheel. Someone said they had gold, which they hadn't—certainly not in quantities to make Coronado and his men and the Viceroy of Mexico and His Majesty Carlos V much richer. The invaders said that they desired nothing but friendship and, of course, good lands on which to settle.

Among their explorations was a side trip commanded by García López de Cárdenas who, with twenty-five horsemen, set out west-ward from the Indian villages on August 25, 1540, and three weeks later arrived at the rim of the Grand Canyon.

With untrained eyes, these newcomers believed it to be three or four leagues across and easy to descend. But, as their chronicler, Castaneda, wrote:

They spent three days trying to find a way down to the river, which from above appeared to be only a fathom wide, although, according to what the Indians said, it must be half a league across.

The descent was found to be impossible, for at the end of these three days Captain Melgosa, with Juan Galeras and another companion, they being the lightest and most agile, undertook to clamber down at a place that appeared to them the least difficult. They kept decending in sight of the men left above until they were lost to view. . . .

At four o'clock in the afternoon they returned, without having been able to reach the bottom because of the great obstacles they en-countered, for what from above had appeared to be easy, proved to be, on the contrary, rough and difficult. They said they had been only a third of the way down, but from the place they reached, the river looked very large; indeed, judging from what they saw, it must be as wide as the Indians had said. The men who remained above estimated

46

that some small rocks jutting out from the wall of the canyon must be about as high as a man; but those who went down swore that when they reached them they were found to be taller than the highest tower of Seville.

Such was the first written description of the Grand Canyon. It must have been doubly vexing to find a canyon with inaccessible depths in an arid region whose Indians possessed little gold. The Spaniards returned home, not without having spilled Indian blood, and having had some of theirs spilled.

But more Spaniards came as the decades passed. Hopi hospitality was met by friendship, but also enmity, greed, and slavery, and the Indians were formally asked to submit to the King of Spain. After enough of this, the men of peace became men of war, and rose in a Pueblo revolt in 1680.

Hopi also turned against Hopi; they themselves massacred the inhabitants of their own village of Awatovi for having collaborated with the intruding Spaniards. They resisted conversion to other faiths and sustained their rituals, withdrawing to their mesa tops as the Spaniards slowly occupied the Southwest and overwhelmed the Pueblo tribes.

And so the prevailing philosophy of the plateau country changed from reverence for natural beauty, to which the Hopis clung and which was the principal philosophy of the incoming Navajo Indians, to the exploitative industrial ethic that nature existed for man, not the other way around.

"We are absolute masters of what the earth produces," said Cicero in his *Tusculan Disputations.* "We enjoy the mountains and the plains. The rivers are ours. We sow the seed, and plant the trees. We fertilize the earth. . . . We stop, direct, and turn the rivers: in short by our hands we endeavor, by our various operations in this world, to make, as it were, another Nature."

Under similar banners much later, newcomers multiplied at the Grand Canyon as elsewhere. Explorers, hunters, trappers, military men, miners, hoteliers, and trail builders arrived—all more or less intent on making another nature that would be obedient to their demands.

An army officer, Lt. Joseph Christmas Ives, explored the lower Colorado River in 1857 and pronounced the Canyon country "profit-less." Some of the earliest men to explore the Canyon did so by boat—James White in 1867 and John Wesley Powell in 1869 and 1871. The telegraph arrived at Pipe Spring, to the north, and shortly

47

afterward the rails of the Atlantic and Pacific, later the Santa Fe, Railroad to the south.

The men of most profound perception were the early geologists, and none wrote with greater eloquence than Clarence E. Dutton, an army officer who was with Powell's scientific surveys of the plateau region in the 1870's.

The Grand Cañon of the Colorado is a great innovation in modern ideas of scenery, and in our conceptions of the grandeur, beauty, and power of nature. . . . The lover of nature, whose perceptions have been trained in the Alps, in Italy, Germany, or New England, in the Appalachians or Cordilleras, in Scotland or Colorado, would enter this strange region with a shock, and dwell there for a time with a sense of oppression, and perhaps with horror. . . .
But time would bring a gradual change. Some day he would suddenly become conscious that outlines which at first seemed harsh and trivial have grace and meaning; that forms which seemed grotesque are full of dignity; that magnitudes which had added enormity to coarseness have become replete with strength and even majesty. . . . Great innovations, whether in art or literature, in science or in nature, seldom take the world by storm. They must be understood before they can be estimated, and must be cultivated before they can be understood.

Dutton was, on occasion, accompanied by the eminent artist Thomas Moran, whose paintings affected the imagination as deeply as did Dutton's words. Through both, the Canyon became well known in scientific circles and to the public at large.

Bills to establish a national park here were introduced as early as 1882 but had little success for more than three decades.

Prospectors arrived. They searched for gold and ultimately left their burros, which later multiplied. Miners staked their claims, housing themselves in overhangs, huts, or simple rock shelters. They built trails, bridges, and tramways, and when the mining proved to be too far from market to be profitable, they turned to the more lucrative tourist trade, established themselves as guides and built hotels, the first in 1884.

Tourists came by horse and by buggy. Stagecoach runs began.

Most visitors reacted in a predictable fashion. They were stunned by the Canyon. "No matter how far you have wandered hitherto," said John Muir, the great Sierra Nevada naturalist, "or how many famous gorges and valleys you have seen, this one, the Grand Canyon

The Little Colorado River runs through Indian country.

of the Colorado, will seem as novel to you, as unearthly in the color and grandeur and quantity of its architecture, as if you had found it after death, on some other star; so incomparably lovely and grand and supreme is it above all other canyons. . . ."

The paraphernalia of civilization grew: resort camps, a school, corrals, tents, an orchard, cattle, sheep, a post office, more hotels, stores, studios, rubbish heaps. . . .

A spur of the Santa Fe Railroad reached the canyon in 1901, automobiles in 1902.

To halt a little of this pell-mell "progress," President Benjamin Harrison created the Grand Canyon Forest Reserve by proclamation in 1893, and then Theodore Roosevelt proclaimed the area a game reserve in 1906. This gave protection to some wildlife, but not to all, especially not to predators, which were at the time presumed to be a serious threat to other wildlife in the region. The fact that predators and prey had evolved together for thousands of years before man came, and that each group of animals was actually beneficial to the other, was largely disregarded in that day.

At this point Congress was trying to decide whether private enterprise or the government itself should operate the facilities and transportation systems that were proliferating in and around the Canyon. Some Congressmen felt that more and more tourists should come to the Canyon; one even approved of making the Canyon another Coney Island because that way more people would get to see it.

As always, engineers obliged these desires, and stood ready to tackle any scheme. A man named Robert Brewster Stanton had already run the river and surveyed a route that would have carried a railroad through the Grand Canyon along the Colorado River.

After 1900, a group called the Grand Canyon Scenic Railway Company proposed to construct some tracks along the rim for a distance of twenty-five miles between El Tovar Hotel and Grandview Point. The only way of making that trip was along a dusty, dirty, and sometimes muddy wagon road that required four hours to traverse and was closed for most of the winter on account of weather. Most people agreed that Grandview Point offered one of the most spectacular views from the south rim, for from there, thrust out into the Canyon, one could see many miles in nearly every direction.

The rim railroad would not only be faster and eliminate dust and mud, it would provide more continuous viewing of the canyon all the way out to Grandview. Built fifty to a hundred feet back from the rim it would, of course, require the removal of some of the forest. Proponents of the plan, however, described this forest as "no timber to amount to anything other than that of scrubby and straggling growth."

The track would have been complete with cindered roadbed and a sidewalk for pedestrians, and the cars to be used on it would have been gasoline powered.

At the same time, plans were completed to tunnel 3,000 feet at a 45-degree angle down through solid rock from the hotel to Indian Gardens, an oasis visible below the village, construct a loop railroad out across the Tonto Platform to the brink of the inner gorge, and then build an elevator for the last 1,500 feet to the river.

Tempting as this might have been, for numerous persons genuinely wished to show off this great wonder to as many people as they could, Congress held back, and the President veered away from such a course. Roosevelt established Grand Canyon National Monument on January 11, 1908, a move which railroad proponents felt was designed to circumvent their plans.

Everyone seemed to feel that a road had to be built along the rim sooner or later, allowing access to more than just a couple of viewpoints. But the United States Forest Service, which assumed administration of the monument because the entire area of about 800,000 acres had been carved out of Coconino National Forest, had the responsibility. And sometimes, with responsibility goes prudence.

"It is of the utmost importance in all considerations," said a 1909 Forest Service report, "to keep in view the fact that the national monument holds doubtless the greatest masterpiece of world sculpture, and as such it is the duty of the Federal Government to maintain and protect it against all forms of private enterprise which would in any degree interfere with the general use and benefit of the public at large."

Whether to admit automobiles became a lively issue. The Forest Service said that the danger of accidents on scenic roads along the rim was too great even to consider the idea. Nevertheless, progress, as it was called in those days, continued, and automobiles were allowed to enter. One by one, some of the earlier iniquities were reduced or eliminated. In August, 1916, Congress established the National Park Service to administer a sprawling system that had been growing helter-skelter since creation of the world's first national park—Yellowstone—in 1872.

The act establishing Grand Canyon National Park was signed by President Wilson on February 26, 1919. According to this act, the canyon was dedicated and set apart as a public park for the benefit and enjoyment of the people. It was also made subject to the provisions of the act of August 25, 1916, by which the National Park Service had been established. Hence, in effect, the Canyon came under two laws, and the act of 1916 actually said more about how the Canyon would be administered than did the act that established the park.

We are obliged to consider the wording carefully. The Service thus established, said Congress in the act, "shall promote and regulate the use of the Federal areas known as national parks, monuments, and reservations hereinafter specified by such means and measures as conform to the fundamental purpose of the said parks, monuments, and reservations, which purpose is to conserve the scenery and the natural and historic objects and the wild life therein and to provide for the enjoyment of the same in such manner and by such means as will leave them unimpaired for the enjoyment of future generations."

These stand as the central words of a mandate by which the Grand Canyon survives. They are anomalous and contradictory, and some even say they are impossible to apply because they require both use and preservation, which at times are held to be incompatible. But as often happens with such glowing landmark statements, the problem has lain not in the words of the act but in the interpretation of them by subsequent generations.

It is difficult to suppose that the framers of this act knew what they were getting into with that word "unimpaired."

Or that Theodore Roosevelt fully realized how difficult human restraint would prove to be when he spoke the following words at the Canyon on May 6, 1903:

In the Grand Canyon, Arizona has a natural wonder which, so far as I know, is in kind absolutely unparalleled throughout the rest of the world. I want to ask you to do one thing in connection with it in your own interest and in the interest of the country—to keep this great wonder of nature as it now is. I was delighted to learn of the wisdom of the Santa Fe railroad people in deciding not to build their hotel on the brink of the canyon. I hope you will not have a building of any kind, not a summer cottage, a hotel, or anything else, to mar the wonderful grandeur, the sublimity, the great loneliness and beauty of the canyon. Leave it as it is. You can not improve on it. The ages have been at work on it, and man can only mar it. What you can do is to keep it for your children, your children's children, and for all who come after you, as one of the great sights which every American if he can travel at all should see. We have gotten past the stage, my fellow-citizens, when we are to be pardoned if we treat any part of our country as something to be skinned for two or three years for the use of the present generation, whether it is the forest, the water, the scenery. Whatever it is, handle it so that your children's children will get the benefit of it.

5

RANGER DAYS

WHAT WAS THIS entity thus taken over as a national park?
Mortal man, so presumptuous, had assumed the management of
a section of the earth's surface about which he knew very little and
dedicated himself to keeping it undisturbed.

With knowledge too rudimentary for a task so enormous he had
embarked upon the management and administration of an area that
included not only a colorful canyon and the fauna and flora that
belonged in and around it but also the air, the silence, the solitude,
the spell and "romance," and even the sky.

At first, perhaps, only protection was meant. Law enforcement,
at least, was within the competence of man. He had had some experience and training in keeping his fellow men from obstructing the
law and defacing the countryside.

Even that task was trying. The rangers stopped or slowed the
shooting, building, marring, destroying, taking objects away, and
other subversion of the purposes for which the park and the National
Park Service were established. That mandate lay undeniably within
the rangers' capacity; it was urgent and could be duly and legally
exercised (although even the rangers killed predators in Grand
Canyon until 1931).

Yet where in the Code of Federal Regulations, which so ably deals
with speed and weight limits on highways, were there limits established on defacement of silence? Where among rules of construction
were rules on constriction of the emptiness, or indeed destruction of
the sky?

Such seeming abstractions had been of little moment before. They
had not existed earlier, or no one had paid attention as time went on.

Besides, men felt—and it would probably be surprising how many still feel—that God had made this Canyon for their exclusive use.

Quotations were legion about this Canyon's being the handiwork of the Creator. Each day after we opened the rim museum for reception of visitors, we could always expect to hear a dozen times or more the comment that the Canyon made man feel so small; that it showed how truly there was a God.

Some visitors felt a possessive interest and brought friends back again and again to see the Canyon. And many indeed recommended that everyone else in America see this sight, as Theodore Roosevelt had said. In this Canyon lay a few of the roots of patriotism.

Here, too, were the roots of beauty, inspiration, love, wonder. There were many reasons expressed as to why one should return, and why others should come. To get the most out of life. For fulfillment. For spiritual renewal. For contact with God. For perspective.

Whatever the reason, people came: 67,300 in 1920; 172,800 in 1930; 371,600 in 1940; 665,000 in 1950; 1,186,900 in 1960; and more than two million in 1970.

Thus it became quite clear that men entrusted with the job of taking care of this complex area would have to divide their activities into two segments: taking care of the people and taking care of the park.

Taking care of the people has always meant attention to their safety first. The very existence of any public park is an invitation to enter, but since this national park is an alien world replete with hazards about which men in their customary environment are unaware, they are likely to get into danger without realizing it. Hence the ranger's job included protection of visitors from falling and other accidents, from animals, and from other men.

As park roads and approaches were improved, the automobile came. And from then to now, the behind-the-scenes activity has involved every conceivable—and some inconceivable—acts of men.

Suicides, of course, hurl themselves into the Canyon, but not many; that is one of the least of the ranger's worries. His number one problem is moving-traffic violations. This is a natural consequence of heavy travel on roads designed for traffic much less hectic than that in cities or on freeways. Some travelers, of course, bring their frenzied habits with them and that, together with congestion, produces accidents.

The ranger is confronted with an increasing number of parking violations, violations of the liquor laws, be-ins and love-ins, and he

55

must deal with loitering, theft, vandalism, shoplifting, burglary (twenty cases a year), forcible and unlawful entry (twenty cases a year), larceny over fifty dollars (forty cases a year), and larceny under fifty dollars (seventy cases a year). Such crimes have increased over the years, and some of them are abetted by the urban environment within the park, the congested areas where employees live.

Car clouting—the breaking into or even driving off of a car—can be difficult for the owners when that car is parked at a trail head and they are down the trail. Clouters may jack up a car, take off the two rear wheels, and drop the vehicle back down in the dirt.

We have apprehended visitors picking flowers or digging up cactuses, which is sometimes unintentional vandalism or unwitting violation of law. More malicious vandals lift nature trail labels or stakes out of the ground and fling them into the chasm. Or they shatter the glass of trail exhibits located within the canyon and scatter specimens along the trail.

The confrontation between visitors and deer along park highways causes rapid aging among rangers. Upon spying a buck or doe at the edge of the road, some drivers will stop their cars at once, half on, half off the pavement. Doors burst open and passengers fly out. It takes only a little common sense to see the hazards of this practice, especially when it occurs on curves and, as inevitably happens, a dozen more cars arrive, stop, and their doors fly open.

Collision between moving vehicles and deer is quite common, but the major causes of human fatalities in the park are heart attacks—exertion at 7,000 feet can be dangerous to the unaware—and accidents resulting from reckless driving.

There have been a number of airplane crashes in the park, the worst being a 1956 mid-air collision of two commercial airliners that took 218 lives. Small planes have made forced landings on sand bars along the Colorado River, at the bottom of the Canyon; this is a dangerous feat, to say the least, and can be costly, for the disabled craft must be dismantled and hauled out piece by piece on muleback or by helicopter. And while this book was being written, two helicopters crashed—one in the Canyon and one on the rim—with tragic and horrible loss of life.

Park rangers can talk by the hour of rescue operations to bring out dead and injured. One boy rode his bicycle over the edge. An intoxicated woman fell into the Canyon and, while being carried out,

56

Natural limestone alcoves above the Colorado River.

bit one of her rescuers. Rangers are compelled to search for lost children, puppies, kittens, and even pet monkeys.

The ranger's traditional fighting of fires has not yet ended, but sophisticated techniques have made the job much easier. For example, it is now well known that the major cause of forest fires is lightning, so rangers fly air patrols after electrical storms in order to detect any fires in their early stages.

For genuine emergencies, helicopters in recent years have made it possible to evacuate injured persons more rapidly and safely than before. Where once a rescue crew of ten required five days to bring out a victim, now it can be done by two men in just a few hours—though the degree of danger is still as great to those two men and the noise far more distracting, even if justifiable.

Visits by eminent people sometimes seem simple at first. For example, a famous lawmaker may arrange with a private outfitter to go by boat down the Colorado River. It does not seem necessary to inform the National Park Service. But then the party is swollen with newsmen, aides, friends, and other participants, until the string of mules reserved to carry the group out becomes inadequate, and the party finds that additional mules are already booked by other Canyon travelers.

In this emergency, the superintendent gets urgent requests for helicopter landing operations. Rangers are diverted from their regular duties. Scheduled park operations may have to be altered, deferred, or canceled. Emergency plans are made ready. The Canyon solitude is breached by steady ascents and descents of helicopters.

By the end of the affair, forty people have been evacuated by air, and a string of mules has had to be brought back out of the canyon nearly empty. As often happens in such cases, the superintendent gets publicly criticized for not having planned the operation in an orderly manner, and the concessioner for charging too much for mules not used.

A group of hippies once started rappelling down the side of the Canyon on a two-hundred-foot piece of rope—which severely upset and frightened visitors who gathered to watch.

But what turns the rangers prematurely gray is the frequent sight of unsupervised children running along the edge of the Canyon, or walking or balancing on top of protective railings. Heavy mesh fencing helps a little, but it is simply impossible to try to keep ahead of everyone who dares the Canyon.

Just the thought of climbing Grand Canyon cliffs is enough to chill the marrow of most persons. But park rangers have to be ready to go anywhere and do nearly anything.

They also have to deal with threatened large-scale invasion. One year park rangers learned, through informants and cooperating law enforcement agencies, that several motorcycle gangs were planning to come to the Canyon and stir up trouble. Rumor had it that somewhere between two hundred and two thousand riders would come in on "chopper bikes" armed with shotguns built into the handlebars and knives stashed under the seats.

To most persons this might sound like a dream from *delirium tremens*. To the rangers it sounded entirely possible.

Legitimate family motorcycle groups had been coming to the Canyon in large numbers annually for quite some time, but authorities had finally been compelled to request some limitation of numbers because of increased congestion and excessive noise.

That year, however, word was out that the Labor Day weekend would be more interesting than usual and that tourists might have some real excitement to add to their sightseeing.

Reports continued to spread. One said that the outlaw gangs would arrive in force, carrying a carload of guns in a hearse. Shortly afterward, a secondhand hearse that was in use merely as a passenger vehicle, was stopped at one entrance to the park and inspected thoroughly. The driver remained nonchalant. The same thing, he said, had already happened five times.

The National Park Service decided that it could not afford to take any chances. All available law-enforcement officers in the park were mobilized and sixteen rangers brought in from other parks. Crowd and riot-control squads, made up of carefully trained maintenance employees, were put on standby alert.

As the weekend approached, rangers set up checkpoints at park entrances. All cars were stopped and given a handbill stating that a critical camping situation existed and that all persons who had no accommodations or camp space by nightfall would have to leave. 59

Twenty sheriff's deputies and twenty-five state highway patrolmen arrived. Water trucks were positioned so that they could be pulled across the roads in case an attempt was made to run through any checkpoint, night or day.

Keeping mayhem out of the park was the all-important goal. Rounding up lawbreakers, once they got inside, could be dangerous to innocent bystanders. Even so, special plans were made with

United States marshals for mass arrest, detention, and removal of troublemakers from the park if it should become necessary.

Sure enough, the motorcycle gangs arrived, their progress across Arizona marked carefully by state authorities. As it turned out, about a hundred and twenty persons came, mayhem and all.

They literally took over a Forest Service campground outside the park, about seven miles south of the rim. Bending over backward to avert disaster, the Forest Service advised all campers of what was happening, enabling them to seek other places to camp.

After the gangs got established, two cars that had accompanied the group collided on the approaches to the campground, resulting in three persons dead and two injured critically. The cars contained leaders of the motorcycle gangs, some of whom were found to be carrying marijuana. The gangs blamed the National Park Service, of course, saying that if the Service had permitted them to enter the park this wouldn't have happened.

Tension mounted. Park rangers were alerted to threats of massed motorcycle brigades running road blocks and invading the park.

The rangers were ready. Their determination that the groups would not enter was about as solid as the granite in the inner gorge. And so the prospect of bloodshed seemed real and clear.

As it happened, the gangs never entered. Labor Day came and went, and so did they. Sheriffs' deputies followed them as they rode out of the state, making sure that their belligerence did not erupt elsewhere. No blood was spilled inside the park, but preparations cost the public treasury $10,000 above the regular park budget, not to mention expenses of sheriffs, patrolmen, marshals, and back-up forces.

Even so, the price could have been much higher—and not just in terms of dollars. Precautions and security made possible the maintenance of serenity for holiday visitors, most of whom knew little or nothing of hidden threats that lay a few miles off through the woods.

Was it a dream? Did it actually happen at the Grand Canyon, where men come to rest and relax, to know the joy in solitude, to evade the cares of urban life, to visit places of beauty and wonder, or listen to lectures that deepen their understanding of primordial times and events?

Bighorns among the fallen strata opposite Elves Chasm.

Like most national parks, Grand Canyon has always been relatively remote. With the improvement of transportation methods and routes, the distance between the Canyon and centers of population has been, in effect, reduced. Through these channels of easy access, the tendency has been, and will continue to be, for urban environments to approach, invade, and conquer wilderness ones. And so it is that disruptive groups should increase along with the growing number of visitors.

Such groups are a minor element, however, of the ranger's concerns, which are oriented primarily toward the comfort, accommodation, transportation, and proper use of the park by visitors in general. A major job is the satisfaction of the public's will to know. Most persons want only to see and, having seen, to go away.

Some want only simple information: where this is and where that is, how far it is over to that place, whether those are horses in the bottom, whether Chinese sculptors really carved those buttes with Chinese names, where the rest rooms are, how far it is to Las Vegas, what that clump of yellow flowers was along the road, what kind of seeds these are, what rangers do in winter, what state you are from, and whether you know some people in Tupelo by the name of—

Some, perhaps fewer than 10 per cent of all visitors, have a real and persistent desire to go beyond the acquisition of information and enter the realm of understanding and appreciation. These people want to know not only how big the Canyon is but also how it got so big, why it is there in the first place, how the river cut it, how the elements widen it, and something about the delicate ecosystem that covers it like a fragile skin and penetrates its deepest corners.

For them, the Canyon is virtually a field-research center in biological and geological sciences. It has self-guiding nature trails, museums, road and trail exhibits, books and booklets, daily talks by naturalists, and in the summer, daily walks and nightly campfire programs that extend the visitor's knowledge beyond the dimensions or distances most often asked about.

62

A natural science laboratory has been built up by some of the most competent geologists, biologists, and generalists in the country. Over forty years of steadfast accumulation of data, specimens, and written records have resulted in a workshop and study station almost without parallel in any of the world's twelve hundred national parks and equivalent reserves.

In it are study collections of plants, reptiles, insects, mammals, birds, fishes, the invertebrates, amphibians, rocks, fossils, minerals, and historical and archeological remains. Observation records contain eyewitness data accumulated for decades by rangers, naturalists, maintenance men, and others who have reported strange and unusual, as well as regular, comings and goings of things in the wild world. And for anyone who wishes to ponder more deeply than others, a splendid library houses volumes of journals, reports, and other works that may open up new domains and take the visitor into another world, another time.

The second task of the ranger, after caring for people, is caring for the park. Originally, this involved the shelter, protection, destruction or removal of plant and animal species thought to be harmful, control of wild fire, and even removal of predators to "improve" deer herds— all of which, considering the knowledge and philosophy of that time, seemed the right thing to do.

That this wilderness had been functioning for millenniums before man came, and had evolved into a fluctuating but apparently quite stable ecological balance, was not fully recognized. Men thought they were protecting the forest by stopping the fires that burned in it. But fires had burned there for thousands of years.

Men thought they could improve deer herds by eliminating the mountain lion. They imagined that thousands of head of cattle could be supported on those rich wild meadows outside the present park, where forage looked so nutritious and abundant.

Once again men attempted to change an environment to fit their own concept of what it ought to be like. And, as a result, the wild-life suffered, the meadows suffered, and the environment changed not toward a Utopia that men might have envisioned, but toward an unwanted desert.

That trend was reversed with establishment of the park, an indication of man's change from the will to conquer to the resolve to conserve.

Yet still he did not know a great deal about conserving it. He had had to spend too much time staving off attacks such as those by dam builders, who would inundate portions of the Canyon.

The minuscule amounts of money received for operations research didn't help very much and most of the time there weren't any. Nevertheless, park naturalists made records and pictures and began to analyze troubling situations from an ecological point of view. Biologists and geologists worked for many a summer, and on the foundation of their work the park education (interpretive) program expanded.

But the question still remained and continued to grow: whether man was powerful enough, learned enough, or wise enough to keep this Canyon "unimpaired." There was a concern—faint at first, or overshadowed by the reservoir controversies, but growing stronger—that man could damage this Canyon, would damage it, without knowing why or without being able to foresee the final result of his actions.

In short—whether men really understood the Canyon.

And of course this led to the question of what a man would have to do to gain an insight into the mysteries of nature so long withheld from the human mind. Perhaps it was necessary for him to listen to the voices of the wind again and hear the message they conveyed. Or to become reacquainted with the silence, the solitude, the emptiness.

Or to understand the sky.

In those days the happiest sight was the lone hiker going off down the trail, enveloped by a wilderness about which he would understand a great many things that had been dark to him before, and where perhaps he would come to learn a great deal more about himself.

6

WHISPERING TREES

TRANSEPT CANYON had turned almost black. We raced through the forest to see what was going on, and presently burst out through the trees and stood at the edge.

A powerful gust of uprushing wind nearly hurled us back into the woods. The Canyon had almost disappeared. Only a fuzzy, viscous haze to the left, vaguely lighted from behind with hues of red and yellow, hinted that there was a Grand Canyon at all.

The rest was black and roiling. Great thunderheads that had been boiling up all morning now obscured the sky. Their surging, seething masses had lowered, dimming the sun and blotting it out, then turning the sky from blue to gray. The north rim, at 8,200 feet elevation, was surrounded by clouds.

Park visitors had seen the storm coming and withdrawn to their tents or rooms or the sheltered terrace of the lodge. They had fled from the storm, to insulate themselves and hide from its vicissitudes and dangers. We went forth to meet it. We went to hear its intricate orchestration, to see its drama played out over the gorge below, to get wet, to participate in the event. We did not want to be merely spectators or refugees.

The Grand Canyon was about to explode. The sounds we heard were the introductory music to an Olympian tempest. Men who thought that little, if anything, ever stirred these regions, would now find out.

The wind picked up dust, swirled it in space, and drove it into our eyes and ears. We tasted it. We washed it away with tears. We held our hands up instinctively, but there was no escaping it. Dust came from everywhere with whirlwind intensity—from the depths below, from the rim at our feet, from the forest behind.

Leaves and twigs broke away from the thrashing oaks and aspens and joined the spinning circle. Down to the ground or up into the sky in long sweeps, the unleashed wind blew this way and that, never predictable, always erratic, feinting and thrusting, interspersing its attack with almost eerie spells of calm.

From trees on the rim came sounds like the playing of a thousand strings: pine needles strummed by pulses of the wind. Flexible trees bent and thrashed to the breaking point, and now and then an old limb snapped and crashed to rock or earth below.

All around the giant amphitheater below, throughout the darkening void of the Transept, the invisible arms of the wind thrashed other trees and drew special music from the pinyons and junipers at lower elevations. This different sound could be distinguished even in all the melee. During moments of the wind's withdrawal, a sound of muted strings from below came clearly up the gorge. In fact, there seemed to be another register, like the lower manual of an organ, playing an accompaniment we could not quite follow.

But it was there. It gave the scene a feeling of distance and depth, of differing levels of action, of rapid movements and powerful forces at work.

The clouds overhead seethed like a massive waterfall. They opened and closed. They leaped up in curls and waves. They swirled into formless masses or tumbled chaotically right and left like the flying mane of a galloping stallion.

As we watched, they turned ominously green, a sign of severe inner violence and very likely the manufacture of hail. By now the trees on the opposite side of the Transept were becoming obscure, and we knew that rain had begun to sweep into the gorge. The clouds were unleashing their floods.

A blinding shaft of lightning connected one of the points just opposite with the grinding electric circuits in the clouds above. The discharge was like that across a capacitor, only here the scale was earth-size, sky-size. For an instant, perhaps as long as a second or two if you count the persistent image that remained on the retina, the turbulent scene exploded in a bright white flash. The Canyon colors leaped into view—gray, dull red, dark brown, soft tan—but pale and unearthly as in fluorescent light.

Darkness returned more intensely than before. Then came the shock of thunder, an instant crash, snapping as though a hundred giant pines had broken at once; then the sound divided into many pieces and the tone of it fell quickly into a bass rumble, as though a shipment of giant marble cubes had been unloaded on the stairs to Jupiter's temple and were tumbling freely, noisily, ponderously down to earth and then bouncing over the edge and clattering into the Canyon.

Echoes came from every corner of the Transept, and from the bottom of the chasm, then rolled away to the central canyon in the mist-filled distance, and simultaneously seemed to come from all directions, stereo-fashion, in and out of the forest.

The whole rim seemed to shake. It seemed quite possible that the rocks would split under such an assault or that the trees would be uprooted in some tumultuous cataclysm that almost certainly lay at hand. In his most fanciful imagination an observer could expect a maelstrom to open up and engulf him and the forest and all living things, and the clouds and rain, and pull them into the underworld that the Hopis revered so much, leaving only the eternal walls and rims of the Canyon to surround the void.

But as quickly as it came, the image disappeared. The drawn-out rumble of the vanishing thunder continued to echo through every chamber within the Canyon. From this ravine and that, from side canyons, back canyons, deep canyons, hidden canyons, came one roll after another answering the master thunderclap.

What music it was! Surely Thor never had a better chamber in which to strike his hammer.

We stood transfixed. Though long drawn out, the thunderous echoes vanished far too soon. We hoped for a replay, so that we could hear again the joyous rapture of the sky cut loose. We were not disappointed, for once more came the lightning, and again the crack and the boom and the roll. . . .

Rain now plunged in heavy sheets. Water sweeping on the winds flew into our faces with a refreshment unlike any other. Clean and clear and borne on the tides of turbulence, the rain came again and again, swirling into the trees, drenching them and us, spilling its cool waters everywhere. Our vision was nearly blanked out. The clouds and shadowed rim melted into a blur, but the flashing light continued.

For the sake of safety we retreated to an overhang and from there watched the consummation of the tempest. For twenty minutes there was no cessation of the intensity of the storm. Shortly after it began, as we had anticipated from the greenness of the sky, hail began

67

to fall. White pellets, about the size of marbles, beat a tattoo as they smashed against the trunks of trees or into the white rim rock and broke into a hundred pieces.

All about us balls of ice bounced around like popcorn in a popper, rolled into crevices, or disappeared over the rim. In no time they had accumulated into tiny drifts, painting the forest floor with strands of white.

As the roar of the storm diminished, the roar of the flood increased. Rain came down by buckets full. The collected waters poured over the edge of the canyon and disappeared into the emptiness.

The sky grew brighter. Color slowly returned. The rain abated. Lightning played farther up toward the summit of the plateau. Thunder sent an occasional echo through the trees or up from the open chambers below. The wind died. The trees stopped thrashing.

Pools and lakes had formed across the forest floor. Yellowish water poured into and out of each. Rivulets coalesced into streams that plunged over the edge. Cascading waters fell into talus slopes of black organic soil and thereafter became little more than tumbling torrents of mud.

Now a new sound lifted above the roar as birds came back to the soaking, dripping trees. A Steller's jay, pent up for nearly an hour, burst out with a screech that none of the new waterfalls could drown. A hawk flew out of the forest and over the void, alert to scampering mammals flooded from their homes.

The whole forest possessed a zest and zip of freshness. Nature awakened once again and reassured each living thing that had taken refuge from the storm.

By now, however, there was little doubt that the upper walls of the Canyon were on the move. The red, brown, and black waterfalls attested to that. Away from the overhang and walking along the rim we scanned the slopes with binoculars and counted hundreds of cascades. Rocks rolled along and fell over one cliff after another. Earth and soil were absorbed or torn away and flung down the slopes or fanned out over the terraces.

68

Here and there collections of debris overflowed a natural spillway and surged into clumps of oaks or against a pinyon pine. By nightfall any number of trees or shrubs might have the soil completely washed away from their roots, and if they were not anchored firmly into the rock itself, they, too, could tumble over the edge.

Canyon cactus patches are numerous and extensive.

At a time like this, storms obviously did great violence to soils unprotected by vegetation. Thorough soaking lubricated the rocks that reposed at precarious angles. With underpinnings loosened, whole slopes fell away, with a resulting landslide spilling tons of rock and debris into the gorge below.

Perhaps at that very minute a distant slump was blocking off some portion of the hiking and riding trails. Indeed, where rivulets converged they often formed steep rivers that madly tore out everything in their paths. If the storm had unloaded the bulk of its moisture over a single basin, or the watershed of a single stream system, the mouth of that system would have some devastating floods.

Telephone communications might well be out at that moment, cut by one or another aspect of the storm. Dinner would be by candlelight tonight if the power lines were damaged. Water would be rationed if the pipes that climbed from Roaring Springs, 3,800 feet below, had been broken by flooding debris.

And out in the forest, as yet unseen, the passage of lightning had doubtless left a trail of smoldering snags or smoking duff. As time went on the heat would intensify. Smoldering debris would turn into burning debris when the dry mountain air took away the moisture of the rain. And then, in days to come, a flare-up would occur in a tinder-dry forest, and wildfire would be under way, repeating the sequence of centuries. Then another spectacle would begin: the roaring of fire, the crash of timber, the fleeing of wildlife. Once more this wilderness would be on the move.

For thousands of years this has happened repeatedly, no telling how many times. Perhaps a million floods and a million fires have swept across this plateau and to its edge and within the gorge. Each one has thinned the forest, changed or enriched the soil, eliminating the weak among trees and animals. Each has shaped the future of certain seeds that have become dependent upon the grinding action of floods or the searing heat of fires.

70   Such was the forest we lived in on the north rim, a forest bathed in flood and baptized in fire for millenniums before men got there. Yet coincident with all that violence, it had grown into one of the most beautiful and richest forests in the world.

Now in late afternoon, the black clouds rolled away. The electric releases were now from cloud to cloud, and we had no trouble distinguishing them from the more deadly air-splitting kind between ground and cloud. The lesser lightning seemed more distant, more chambered, more incoherent; its echoes seemed to ramble among all the tributary canyons.

Over the desert plains tonight would be a storm. But we were free. Only fragments of cloud remained in the sky, together with a high haze. Most of the sky had been rainwashed.

The Canyon came into view again, as sharp and crystal clear as it ever gets. Cloud wisps remained within the gorge, creating and dissolving in an ambience of high humidity.

We watched them until dark, watched the cloud bits curling in and out among the buttes, rising in serpentine trails across the edges of cliffs, creeping among agaves and yuccas that clung to the outer rocks, and pouring over the rim and into the forest with the vanishing atmospheric turbulence of the storm.

Those last few moments of sunlight revealed a resplendent Canyon. The seething and surging waters, for all their silt, had cleaned the land. The Canyon was fresh again! What spirit could not rejoice?

Now the springs would be replenished. The lakes and ponds would be aerated. Life would surge with vigor again. The solid weeks of June—without clouds, without rain, without anything but a burning sun—had ended. Any seeds waiting to be touched with the spark of life would spring forth. The layer of leaves that had lived in other years now had a fragrant odor of freshness. From their decay would come the fullness of new lives.

The storm had gone, but its final delicate nuances would be remembered as well as the music of the puddles and the racing white stallions. That night, raindrops landed now and then on our roof, shaken from the leaves of the aspen trees that overhung the cabin. The silence was glorious. There was no other sound. Off in the distance, the sky displayed a periodic glow that came from somewhere far over the horizon. Not even the sound of thunder could be heard. But the echoes of the afternoon storm remained in our dwindling consciousness, as did the images of thrashing trees and swirling clouds.

Those images would return again and again, reminding us that all was well with the natural world.

71

Some persons say that after spending a summer on the north rim, you can just about live anywhere, for everything thereafter is anticlimactic. Of the many paradises on terra firma, none is quite like this.

Because it is more than a thousand feet higher than the south rim, this part of the Grand Canyon has a much different climate. The summit of the Kaibab Plateau, some miles back from the rim, reaches up to more than 9,000 feet. Of course, the same wet and dry seasons coincide in the general climate of the region, but here the average annual precipitation amounts to nearly thirty inches and in severe winters there may be as much as 350 inches of snow—almost thirty feet. For this reason the highest portions of the north rim are virtually uninhabited by man during half of the year.

Rains begin around the fourth of July and occur reliably throughout the summer. For a while they issue forth every afternoon, then every night for a while. Then comes a period of no storms, then back to the afternoon routine.

It is not at all uncommon to observe half a dozen storms at once when you stand on the forwardmost points, such as Cape Royal. Some rise over mountain country near Flagstaff or over the Indian plateaus to the east. But those most intimate develop from great thunderheads that build up over the Kaibab Plateau itself.

On vista points like Cape Royal, watching an approaching storm can actually be a hair-raising experience. With vertical walls plunging thousands of feet, the cape is in effect a giant lightning rod thrust into the sky, its tip not far from the clouds themselves. Thus, it is susceptible to a condition of atmospheric static electricity known as St. Elmo's fire.

When electrified particles float past a metal tip or a ship's mast or a mountain peak, a charge is drawn by means of electric induction. During this phenomenon, known as point discharge, molecules of gas in the air may be ignited. As the region about the point is ionized, a bluish or reddish glow may occur.

At such times, visitors may receive a shock when they reach out to touch someone else on these forward overlooks. Naturalists see it happen several times a summer: blue streaks of lightning connect one visitor with another, even though the people may be an inch apart. A loud snap may be heard, but neither person is harmed beyond sudden surprise.

Another effect is that with proper consistency and looseness, the hair of human beings stands on end. There are legends, of course, about the lovely young Dianas who flouted their beauty and elegant hairdos all the way to Cape Royal, only to have the arrangement

Rain veils the view from Cape Royal.

come undone in a supercharged atmosphere. The ladies in distress rush back to bus or car with every strand flying outward like the rays of a sun.

This may sound laughable, but the condition can be fairly dangerous, and visitors could well be struck by lightning. When they see sparks flying near them, they ought to decide that, for the moment at least, they have had enough sightseeing on the rim.

There is never a dull moment on the north rim. From that first day when we drove out of the searing heat of House Rock Valley and entered the Kaibab Forest, we became aware of the extraordinary biological richness of the region. Above the pinyon-juniper association we entered stands of ponderosa pine, and almost at once saw one of the Kaibab Plateau's most famous residents, the white-tailed squirrel.

This species is closely related to the Abert squirrel, so closely that both may have once been a single race. But because earth movements lifted the north side higher than the south, the climate here became more severe. The vegetation evolved into a different community. As time went on, each species of squirrel, separated from the other by the widening gulf of the Canyon, went its evolutionary way.

Kaibab squirrels developed dark underparts instead of light, and white tails instead of gray. Today the 220,000 acres of ponderosa pine forest in which they live is entirely surrounded by lowland vegetation, chiefly desert, which does not appeal to them at all and which they are not adapted to live on.

No other white-tailed, tassel-eared squirrels exist. This is their only home, and if anything happens to the twigs, the seeds, the mushrooms on which they sometimes feed—in short, if anything damages the ecosystem—the white-tails could be seriously affected.

They already are. Their population fluctuates. Let the vigor of the forest diminish, and the number of squirrels decreases. Let the stability of the ponderosa community be upset by too many people, too many cattle, too many wood beetles, too much sediment in the air, and the current population of three thousand squirrels could vanish without man's having touched them.

John Muir was right; everything in this universe is hitched to everything else.

74

From Bright Angel Point: Deva, Brahma and Zoroaster Temples, the south rim, and the San Francisco Peaks volcanic field.

The tassel-eared squirrels have for millenniums shared their domain with goshawks, mule deer, mountain lions, coyotes, mice, weasels, porcupines, other squirrels, and many additional animal species. Now they are sharing it with man, who has demonstrated that he can, by simple or selfish or sometimes well-meaning actions, be more of a hazard to these creatures than all the predators in the woods. The mortality on the highways—the crushed carcass with flattened white tail—is a minor but obvious example.

In other respects, man has regarded this plateau with a sense of humor and admiration, as demonstrated by the names he has applied to features on the surface of it. There are Pleasant Valley, Billy Sink, Tater Ridge, Snipe Hollow, Joes Mud Hole, Fracas Lake, Pigeon Pockets, and Wildcat Canyon.

For that matter, the whole of the Grand Canyon and its rims has provided a field day for the exercise of that familiar human passion— the naming of things. Buttes, pinnacles, terraces—everything has a label. More than twenty viewpoints are named after Indian tribes, a dozen side canyons after rocks and minerals, and more than two dozen features after plants and animals. Some topographic features have received Chinese, Hindu, or Egyptian names, and some the elements of neighboring Indian languages: Tatahatso Point, Sase Nasket, Parissawampitts Canyon, Chikapanagi Mesa, and Matkata- miba Rapids.

Many names are so American, so Western, so folkloric that they contain a capsule summary of both the history and romance of the region: Crazy Jug Point, Mount Spoonhead, SB Point, Dead Horse Mesa, Haunted Canyon, Phantom Fault, the Inferno, Tilted Mesa, Sinking Ship, Cathedral Stairs, Hades Lake, Saddle Canyon, and Cape Solitude.

As we climbed higher in elevation, it became apparent that spring comes late on this lofty plateau. Fresh green grass grew in the forest, on meadows, down steep ravines, up rolling ridges. Banks of blue lupine added color to the somber brown of the pine needles.

76

As we gradually reached 9,000 feet, we passed denser, more luxuri- ant forest, mixtures of blue and Engelmann spruce, groves of Douglas fir and white fir. Masses of aspen presented their shimmering leaves to the sunlight and, back-lighted, resembled waves of yellow-green light rolling into the somber shadows of spruce. Some groves, caught in pockets of long winter coolness, had not even begun to leaf out, and though it was June, we passed snow banks that measured three hundred yards in length by thirty feet across.

It is difficult to remember all the adventures that piled on adventures that summer, but the overwhelming majority took place within this gracious forest. From the very first moment, we knew how different was the air itself: clear and fresh, sharpened by cool temperatures, thinned by elevation, redolent with the scent of spruce and fir mixed with the fragrances of a hundred or more kinds of flowers.

To make scientific collections, we often went on trips afield, exploring the quiet vales and shady glens, pushing through tall grass intermingled with youthful pine, spruce, and fir.

One special project involved the collection of wild mushrooms. Cool ravines and moist north-facing slopes offered excellent habitats for their growth. We poked in and under decaying logs, in the deep, soft mat of aspen leaves and among the collected needles of pine and fir.

Some mushrooms barely showed above the surface, so that it took a sharp eye to see them. Others were conspicuous—bright yellow, red, purple, orange. Some were black, others white. The deadly amanita was ever-present. Many mushrooms grew among the tall and delicate death camas at a spring near Cape Royal. There seemed no end to the variations in size and shape; a few had delicate fronds that gave the appearance of coral on a sea floor.

These explorations took us into extensive groves of aspen, white-barked kin to the cottonwood tree, which here represents the transient member of the forest community. The aspen does not remain; it comes into openings made by fire or infestation, and grows as long as spruce and fir do not surround it. At the same time it protects and shelters their growth, so that in time they crowd it out and succeed to a forest climax community, one in which the spruce and fir predominate.

We never ceased to enjoy these explorations. The aspen leaves formed a carpet and in places were covered with glistening sap that was exuded from growing leaves and sprinkled on the ground. Underbrush and dead logs were scattered about, and Kaibab limestone outcropped here and there.

It was a world unto its own, part of an ecosystem unlike any other in the Grand Canyon region.

By the time summer elsewhere came to be half over—that is, well along in July—the wild flowers of the north rim burst out in profusion. Most prominent were red and orange penstemons that grew on rocky slopes. On the Point Imperial drive grew hybrid penstemons in combinations of blue and red. Gilias added brilliance and color; the first ones were a vivid scarlet, and then the roads came to be lined with a handsome pink variety.

Flowers grew everywhere. We walked among phlox that spread their pinkish flowers across the open meadows. We hiked past purple asters, yellow rubber plants, sunflowers, dark-purple flax, white and yellow chickweeds and cryptanthas, and clumps of bluebells.

Wild buttercups and strawberries added a stunning yellow to the meadows, and soon the delicate lavender of harebells took over. Off the Saddle Mountain fire road we saw the rare and fragile Calypso, an orchid.

From late in June to early August the New Mexican locust was by far the most appreciated forest tree because it burst into bloom with brilliant clusters of light pink flowers not unlike sweet peas. These giant legumes graced the sides of roads and trails, and grew in open forest stands as well as in sheltered canyon coves. Their densely flowered racemes often were so heavy they seemed to bend the tree over with added weight.

If anyone ever asks about the best time of year on the north rim, we would have to call a tossup between July, the month of the locust, and October, the month of aspen color.

The locust frequently grows in association with Gambel oak. Where they form thickets, especially on old trails, a hiker rarely passes through, owing not a little to the impressive thorns of locust.

On guided walks, both oak and locust captured considerable attention because they grew so abundantly along the rim. One morning a naturalist leading one of these walks pointed out that such trees served the important function of tying down the soil and reducing erosion along the Canyon rim.

"Well," said an alert young lady in the group, "isn't it a little late to worry about that now?"

Few permanent streams drain the Kaibab Plateau, because the porous rock that caps it absorbs a great deal of water from melting snow and pouring rain. The limestone is pocked with solution pits, or sink holes, some of which have silted up and now hold ponds. We made small collections of aquatic life from these ponds—dragonflies, water beetles, striders, and salamanders—and watched their progress through the summer.

78

A grove of aspen on the side of a limestone sink.

Mosses, lichens, and liverworts embellished the forest glades and garnished the springs. We hiked through patches of clover, buckwheat, and buttercup, lunched beside snowberry bushes, and relaxed in the sparse shade of mountain mahogany. Sometimes our boots made deep holes in the soil that had been loosened by tunneling pocket gophers.

On quiet afternoons we watched robins and bluebirds, as well as flocks of ravens, going after crickets and grasshoppers that fed in the meadows. We followed the paths of chipmunks, or traced the adventures of a chickaree squirrel in a Douglas fir. Red-shafted flickers flew among the aspen or hammered on the ponderosa pines. Occasionally we came upon a blue grouse and her brood of fresh-born chicks. One afternoon on Cape Royal we happened upon a mule deer mother giving birth.

Three months was scarcely enough time to get an introduction to this highly productive forest, much less come to know it intimately. Some persons bragged about "how many miles we've come since Saturday," and asked how to see the most in the shortest time.

Most visitors seemed to have planned their trips with care; yet there were some who drove through the fragrant forests with cars air-conditioned and windows up. Most could not break, even temporarily, the habit of eating meals in late evening and early morning—remaining in dining rooms or around camp tents—when nature's greatest performances were being presented in the forest and along the rim.

For example, a concert of bell-like music opens at dusk in quiet woods away from centers of visitor concentration. The music is sometimes high-pitched, sometimes low and hollow, always sliding in a liquid style. On hearing it the brain at first shuts away all other sounds—the chatter of ravens, the sighing of wind through spruce, the rustling of aspen leaves. Up scale and down, the hermit thrush sings as though lent to earth to demonstrate what the music of heaven sounds like.

The bird itself is nondescript, retiring, and rarely seen, but its melodies fill the forest and amplify the solitude. And in a while our sound-receiving centers let in the music of the spruce and the talk of the ravens again.

Long after you leave the north-rim forest and travel to distant places, the song comes back. You cannot remember exactly how it

Storm over the Indian country, as seen from the Kaibab Plateau.

went. It is too complicated for that. But you do remember the feel of it, the perfection of notes, the complex arrangement. And you know that, when you go back to the north rim next time, your dinner is going to be very late.

Many visitors stroll to an overlook or along a rim trail in order to view the changing, deepening colors when the sun sinks into the desert haze. They watch the sunset and, having witnessed the most colorful part of the display, leave. Yet, by departing too soon, they miss the final act of a memorable performance.

One evening we rode out to Cape Royal when all other visitors were coming back, and by the time we got there the point was uninhabited. The late evening sun on the Walhalla Glades had come in through the trunks of the ponderosa pines and illumined the dense banks of lupine that covered so much of the forest floor.

For thousands of years other human eyes must have viewed these glades with different emotions. Evidence shows that Indians more than a thousand years ago lived in family groups on the north rim plateaus, gathering seeds and using various forest products. They built rock dams that held back water and blocked the removal of soil. The water sustained their crops of corn and beans which were raised on hillside garden terraces.

They would have had their own opinion of the canyon itself, as each man does today. They may have had some gods enshrined within the walls, just as modern man has. From the tip of the Walhalla Plateau, Vishnu Canyon drops away at your feet, going almost straightaway toward the inner gorge. It is rimmed by Vishnu and Freya Temples (Freya is the Norse goddess of beauty) on the east, and flat-topped, sheer-walled Wotan's Throne (Wotan is a German god whose name comes to us in Wednesday) on the west.

From Cape Royal the scenery certainly exists on a celestial scale. Eastward lies a vast expanse of Indian country: the Kaibito Plateau, Black Mesa, a western extension of the Painted Desert. Towering Cape Final on this rim and Cape Solitude above the Palisades of the Desert form buttresses for an enormous river avenue. Beyond are the Echo Cliffs, the Little Colorado gorge, and Shadow Mountain. Southward, the Kaibab Monocline rises toward the Coconino Plateau, on which rest the San Francisco Peaks, seventy miles away, near Flagstaff.

The falling sun draws rich, subdued pastels from all these distant landmarks, and from the Supai and Redwall cliffs below. Then shadows that first filled the inner gorge creep up the sides of the cliffs and climb into the sky.

The wind blew as we walked first along the rim and then back into the forest to listen to the music of the pines. The evening breezes came in gusts, and not all the pines sang at once, just as all the voices of a choir may not be in use at a single time, or all the instruments of an orchestra.

As gusts leaped up over the Canyon rim and burst into the forest, the ponderosa pine answered first, in its sepulchral tones, then the pinyon pine. A blast of air shrilled through a cliff rose, then through a juniper and into a dead tree. Each of these instruments, tuned to a separate key, had its own vibrations. Each made its own response to the wind.

One chorus faded in intensity. Another took up the tune. Then all of them seemed for a moment to cease. The wind died away. Silence almost took over.

But a blast of wind, hurled from the outer darkness, sailed through a nearby pinyon pine. This pine raised a different pitch. Another played a higher note. Silence vanished. All trees sang again, and the forest filled once more with a wild music.

In the final minutes of twilight we saw only the dancing silhouettes of the singing trees. Most were thrashing furiously, but a few stood quietly, waiting to be plucked by the fingers of the wind.

Farther inland, back from the rim, the orchestration became more quiet. The treetops still moved, still whispered, still sighed. But the intermissions were longer. Not a branch moved, not a twig, not a needle, not a flower. Somewhere in the distance, faintly, the rest of the orchestra played. Here, the quiet of night seemed about to descend.

The bright pinpoint of Jupiter shone in the sky. On the western horizon, the only color that remained was a faint line of red. We watched it through the silhouettes of pinyon limbs, some of which were horizontal, some vertical, some angled, some laced and criss-crossed in a pattern never orderly or symmetrical.

83

The wind came again. Part of the orchestra played rapidly, as though in the midst of an allegro, while the other played slowly. Darkness blotted out the shaking heads of the trees but the strumming music of the wind went on. We stayed, caught up in the wildness of the moment, attuned to the mysteries of the night.

But then we, too, would go, leaving only the stars to listen.

7

POINT SUBLIME

"OUTRAGEOUS!"

The visitor was not to be consoled.

"You should be compelled to pay for the repairs to my car!"

He had just returned from the fifty-mile round trip by dirt road to Point Sublime, west along the north rim of the Canyon.

"The dirt and dust covered us and got into all our gear. Rocks in the road—big ones, sharp ones, little ones—cut our tires. High centers kept scraping the under side of the car and kept us on edge the whole day.

"We know what it is to be nervous wrecks now. The limbs of the trees were worst of all. I couldn't avoid them. I had to get out of the ruts, and this threw us against the trunks of trees and into the shrubbery. Would you like to come out and see the scratches on my car? I ought to sue the government!"

He turned and stamped away in a huff. A bystander might have supposed that the United States Government was guilty of urging people to visit an overlook of considerable fame, then subjecting them—as it seemed—to the hellish nightmares of going and coming.

Not quite so, however. The road to Point Sublime pleased a great many more than it displeased. We heard more praise of it than damnation. In fact, it became a sort of rallying point for visitors who felt that the wilderness of Grand Canyon had already been altered too much by the comforts and luxuries of man-made installations.

"That's the kind of road my grandfather traveled over in this

An old road through the Kaibab forest.

country years ago," said a local resident. "There wasn't any other way to travel."

"Don't ever pave it," one visitor urged.

"Leave it alone," said another. "There aren't many places where you can get out like that any more."

After listening to comments about the road to Point Sublime for several months, we began to see that those who disliked it were simply unprepared to meet the wilderness on its own terms. They should not have gone in the first place. Or, having gone, they should have taken more time.

Physical punishment to a vehicle is a price for going too fast, but is by far the least significant aspect of the trip. For if a visitor tries to hurry along that road, he misses some extraordinary experiences. The sights and sounds he passes are not to be matched at home. If he tarries here and there, walks through an open glade, pauses while traversing a meadow, stops in the dense forest, and not only looks but sees, not only walks and rides but explores, the enjoyment will outweigh the inconveniences he may have encountered on the road.

On every aspen tree the thick white bark is arranged in folds and cuts, twists, turns, contortions, and sculptural forms that may be subtly lighted by brilliant sun or tamed by gentle shadows. While it can claim to be the most widespread tree in North America, aspen hasn't the stamina to persist. It comes into open places such as the edges of glades and meadows, or takes root after a forest fire, nourished by a soil that is newly enriched with ashes and absorptive of energy in the open sunlight. Its wood, useful for little more than excelsior, lacks the durability of oak. In time it gracefully succumbs to the very spruces it has sheltered.

But spruce can never be as white and intricately patterned, as vividly green and fresh in spring, or as gold in autumn.

September's chilly nights begin to turn the aspen's leaves to a uniform yellow (although sometimes a few red leaves occur), and by October masses of color make the Kaibab Plateau one of the brightest in the American Southwest.

86

The tremulous movements of their leaves, each on a long and slender stem, give rise to multiple ripplings at the demand of the slightest wind. An aspen grove is a cathedral as fine as any built by man or nature. The flutter of one aspen leaf in an autumn glade summarizes a universal story of life, death, and rebirth.

A colony of quaking aspen trees.

As we watch, a thrush flies up to an aspen perch and sings. Where else need we seek a choir?

The earth is rich and black, supporting a busy ecosystem shared by coyotes and Kaibab squirrels, bears and mountain lions. Dwarf junipers shelter mice and chipmunks from the hovering hawk. Out on the open meadows, pink with phlox, swallowtail butterflies move along in a flurry of yellow.

Larkspur, daisy, buttercup, clover—the forest is filled with wild, high-country gardens. The forest floor is strewn with cones and needles of pines, or is being enriched with dead and decaying logs that return to it the nutrients they borrowed in the endless cycle of energy transfer.

It is difficult to say precisely wherein the charm of the sylvan scenery of the Kaibab consists [wrote Clarence E. Dutton].

We, who through successive summers have wandered through its forests and parks, have come to regard it as the most enchanting region it has ever been our privilege to visit. Surely there is no lack of beautiful or grand forest scenery in America, and it is a matter of taste what species of trees are the most pleasing. . . . I suspect that the charm consists in influences far more subtle than these outward forms. The delicious climate, neither cold nor hot, neither wet nor excessively dry, but always exhilarating, is a fundamental condition by virtue of which the body and mind are brought into the most susceptible mood.

At any moment one may expect to round a bend and find a tree freshly fallen across the way. But usually the route is open, and what of the demerits when the road brings us to such a vale as that where crystal waters of Kanabownits Spring make music in the forest? Who cares about chuckholes when there are harebells and strawberries dotting the greenery just beyond?

We descend through ponderosa pine and juniper, pass blooming locust and cliff rose, negotiate a sharp curve, pass out of the dense forest onto an open sagebrush flat, and then see beyond the last of the trees a blue openness that tells us we are getting close to the point.

88

At one side we glimpse the upper walls of a gigantic amphitheater. We cannot begin to see to the bottom of it. By the map we know it as Shinumo Amphitheater, but all the points of reference are straight from King Arthur: Merlin Abyss, Modred Abyss, Elain Castle, Lancelot Point, Guinevere Castle, King Arthur Castle, and Holy Grail Temple. Someone's imagination took a fanciful flight.

There are no swords or armored horsemen to be found down the

Bass Trail along White Creek, but rather the sweet waters of springs, the crumbling ruins of Indian dwellings, and graceful spires that would have amazed Arthur indeed.

In a sense, he would not have been out of place here. A present-day hiker down in those remote depths experiences much the same exaltation of adventure and overcoming of obstacles, perhaps even a little of the quest for immortality.

Along a narrow neck of land that juts well into the Canyon we make our way, then stop the car and get out. The road to Point Sublime seems as nothing now, every curve and hole, every rut and rock a pittance in payment for one of the greatest shows on earth.

We hardly realize that we have been thrust so far forward, and now have the suspicion that what we are about to see will exceed even Arthur's vale:

The scenery of the amphitheaters far surpasses in grandeur and nobility anything else of the kind in any other region [said Dutton], but it is mere by-play in comparison with the panorama displayed in the heart of the cañon. The supreme views are to be obtained at the extremities of the long promontories, which jut out between these recesses far into the gulf. Towards such a point we now direct our steps. The one we have chosen is on the whole the most commanding in the Kaibab front, though there are several others which might be regarded as very nearly equal to it, or as even more imposing in some respects. We named it *Point Sublime*.

We step out as though into a blue enveloping sea of haze, with maroon and purple flooding the emptiness at our feet, and ask: what else *could* he have named it?

With a loud *swish!* a white-throated swift, zooms near the rim and across the sagebrush prairie. Old stalks of agave lean over the edge, testimony to last year's blooming of the century plant.

At an elevation of 7,464 feet we are so high, and are so far out into the canyon, that we have virtually a horizontal view of 300 degrees. The whole south rim is in view, far away and below. To the left the San Francisco Peaks rise from the plateau surface. Mount Trumbull and its range lie to the west. Each of these volcanic fields is sixty-five miles from where we stand, yet we see them clearly. Red Butte, forty miles beyond the south rim, rises up almost in its entirety as seen from here. The Powell Plateau stretches long and wide toward the waning sun.

No other point except Cape Royal is flung so much like a peninsula into the center of the Canyon. As we stand and try to grasp the scene, a light haze modifies each color into soft pastel. The late-afternoon sun gives them a glowing richness.

A tremendous side canyon opens at our left, another amphitheater that begins far into the north rim, deepens rapidly, and broadens out onto the Tonto Platform far below. From there it gives way to an inner canyon bench that extends to the brink of the inner gorge.

Just below the rim stretches a ridge topped by Coconino sandstone, that sheer light-colored cliff that forms a band along the upper canyon walls. The ridge is topped with pinyon pines and juniper, and one wonders about the life down there, life that perhaps has never known the presence of human beings.

Below this lies the red Supai formation. Long promontories of it are capped with outliers of Coconino sandstone which erosion has separated from the parent superstructure under the rim. These pale yellow remnants seem to form the prows of vessels that have cruised into the Canyon void, like lone white ships on a sea of red. Below that some of the buttes are capped with Supai only, which ends in tips and points like the turrets of a battleship.

East, west, and across—from few points can we see so many scalloped amphitheaters in the Redwall limestone. Many of these hollows, almost precisely semicylindric, would hold a whole academy of music. And what a setting! Where overlaid by the Supai, each is superbly red. Where not, their gray walls drop marblelike from the sky to the gentle slopes below. If a choir be placed up there, we would doubtless have music no tabernacle could match.

But then—listen carefully. The acoustics of the chasm bring to our ears the song of a canyon wren. We listen. The song falls down its scale and is gone. We wait for more. The amphitheater has done the job it was made to do. We do not need to import any outside music.

In all the vast space beneath and around us [Clarence Dutton wrote], there is very little upon which the mind can linger restfully. It is completely filled with objects of gigantic size and amazing form, and as the mind wanders over them it is hopelessly bewildered and lost. It is useless to select special points of contemplation. The instant the attention lays hold of them it is drawn to something else, and if it seeks to recur to them it cannot find them. Everything is superlative, transcending the power of the intelligence to comprehend it.

Layers of rock contain biographical sketches of the earth.

For all the prominence of Point Sublime, we see from here less than a third of the Grand Canyon, which by river course measures 217 miles. We find it a little hard to grasp that the width between rims ranges from as few as four miles to as many as eighteen miles, that, from this point, the river lies four miles away in a straight line. We stand almost precisely 1,000 feet higher than the south rim, and 4,000 feet above the river.

Immensity is always there. Movement is always present, too, the forward, downward, outward motion of land toward the terminal sea. Most men do not see this. They view only eternal stillness in the unmoving walls, stability in the ridges, and silence in the dead, dry washes.

But an almost incomprehensible amount of stone has been eroded from this region. Layer after layer has been peeled away, even hundreds of feet of strata that once reposed over where we stand. Stripped away, denuded, washed out, hauled away—the great denudation it has been called.

The process is still going on. And nearly every element of it is visible from Point Sublime. We see but a single moment of modern history. Strata of muds and sands and lime once laid down horizontally and turned to stone are now disintegrating. They have obviously been disintegrating for a long time.

Whether the Grand Canyon is old or young depends on your point of view. To geologists it is still young. They see in this scene one of great dynamic action.

Those gigantic limestone blocks directly at our feet are tipped and ready to fall right off the rim. Great slabs weighing hundreds of thousands of tons, big enough to equal several houses, lie strewn on the steep slopes. Some piled farther down look half as large as a football field. Others remain at a steep angle of repose, yet are ready to roll at any time.

How many fall per century, per year, per day? Only once on our many trips inside the Canyon did we ever hear anything fall; it came as a rifle shot on the way to Cheyava Falls.

But how often we have seen things *slide* into this canyon. That summer storm on the north rim tore loose tons of soil and rock and plunged them into the gorge. Once on a trip out of the Canyon we got caught in a heavy downpour that unleashed muddy torrents over

Shifting sands lie obedient to the wind.

the walls and brought down talus over the trail. Mule riders had to lead their mules by hand around the perilous slumps.

Meltwaters from heavy snows pour off the Kaibab Plateau, pick up silt and sand and debris, and scour their way down to the river as tributary streams, some of which are permanent, some intermittent.

In winter, as we saw on the trek to Cheyava Falls, temperatures vary widely. A considerable amount of snow melts during the daytime, seeps into cracks and crevices and soaks into the soil. With the rapid dropping of temperature at night—the range may at certain sites approach a hundred degrees—the water freezes, expands, opens the crevices a trifle more, loosens more particles or ledges, and otherwise works to split the masses of rock apart.

Fault zones are particularly susceptible to such action. They are areas of weakness where the rocks have been shattered anyway and thus form lines along which erosion is accelerated.

That is why so many side canyons and cross canyons follow fault lines. A geologic map of the Grand Canyon provides convincing evidence that the topography is controlled by underlying structure. The Canyon is crisscrossed by long vertical fractures which manifest themselves in disruption of the horizontal strata. Untrained eyes cannot always pick out these slightly disrupted layers, but they are there.

They have, in fact, helped breach and make passable some of the sheerer cliffs. Down such a breach the Bright Angel Trail decends; on across the Canyon this trail, and later the North Kaibab Trail, follows the conspicuous canyon that has eroded along the Bright Angel Fault.

The irresistible pressure of expanding ice is almost matched by the pressure of expanding roots. These enter cracks and crevices, seeking soil and nutrients, and by enlarging they widen the crevices. With many generations of roots thus growing—grasses, trees, vines, shrubs, and plants that hug the rocks in mats—soil is loosened.

With temperature changes come changes in pressure of the atmosphere, and winds often race along the rims and swoop down into the Canyon with unbounded fury. Spring in the plateau country often brings a steady gale that persists for days. Funneled through passes, narrowed as a river is narrowed when crashing through a narrow canyon, the wind fairly shrieks its way past the ledges and around the rocks and slopes.

94

Deer Creek, near Surprise Valley.

At such times the sturdy pinyons and junipers hold on as long as they can, but soil may be ripped from around their roots, and if they are not attached in crevices, down they go.

The winds gather dust—fine particles of sharp-edged quartz—and with such tiny tools have at least a minor effect as they help to scour and sculpt the cliffs, round off the edges of ridges, clean away accumulations of soil, and in other ways contribute to the general disintegration.

By all these agents the rocks are gradually broken apart. Every day some part of this inexorable process goes on, silently, inconspicuously, little noticed by man. Geologically speaking, the rate of erosion is very rapid. The Grand Canyon is classed as young.

Landscapes elsewhere, coated with layers of dense vegetation, erode more slowly. Here, beneath raw sun and rain and wind, the land, slave to the power of ice and expanding roots, crumbles faster.

When particles and pieces of cliff break away, when boulders tip too far toward the edge and go on over, the law of gravity assumes command. It is always there, always working. Its force pulls the sand away from the wind, the ledge from the cliff, the slab from the slope. It combines with the roiling waters of swollen rivers to tug at the rocks flushed loose by streams. Small banks of soil are torn away from parent slopes. Gravity grips whole cliffs when they are ready, or whole slopes when they are slickened, and flings them to the tributary gorges below.

Thus every speck of sand, every bit of soil, every boulder, and almost every living and growing entity of vegetation or animal life has a single final destiny: to be propelled into the clutches of that master remover of debris—the Colorado River.

Before being dammed upstream, the river used to carry an average of 500,000 tons of sediment daily through the Grand Canyon. This load varied from several hundred tons, at extremely low water, to more than 27 million tons of sediment in a single day.

That crushing load constitutes a cutting force of enormous power. It rasps, files, grinds, and scours out the bed of the stream, thus lowering the bottom of the canyon. The river thereby continues what was started by the rains. It receives what was offered by the wind, broken by ice and roots, and delivered by gravity. Somewhere in this Canyon, and quite often at several places simultaneously, the process continues, day and night, year in, year out, century after century.

How long the Canyon will last under the combined and diligent assault is hard to say. We do not even know how long it has lasted so far. Studies show that the river has eroded away its drainage area at the approximate rate of 6.5 inches per thousand years. But rate of erosion depends upon the hardness of the layers, and we cannot fix with adequate precision how thick were the layers that have long since worn away.

Today the river slowly cuts through durable granite, schist, gneiss, and pegmatite in the central part of the Grand Canyon. It will continue to do so until it reaches sea level, or until new upheavals change the land.

Standing on Point Sublime, we wish that we could come back at intervals of a hundred thousand years in order to see the changes wrought. That pinnacled butte to the west would surely be gone by then. The battleship below might be reduced to a hulk. Those sailing vessels that have floated out from the rim over there might be dismasted, if not dismantled.

King Arthur's castle could be only a mound. Excalibur might be gone. And Modred's Abyss would be wider.

Thus, all before us is in a state of change. It looks in repose but is not. Today is only a moment in the long adventure of wind and rain.

We stand a long time on Point Sublime, caught in the quiet and calm that must have existed for so long in this region, first during sedimentation on ancient plains and deltas or in primeval seas, and then during uplift so gentle the layers retained their horizontality. This "levelness," only occasionally disrupted by dips and folds, is the essence of the scene from Point Sublime. One layer, one chapter of time, lies on another. Few places on earth reveal so much at a glance or have been cut into so deeply. And if the river has revealed how it cut into the Grand Canyon in the first place, men still disagree on the clues. Was the river there originally, on a low-lying plain? And did the land rise around it? Or could a stream have cut through from the western side and captured the young Colorado?

There is much yet to be learned. The evolution of the river may be as hard to resolve as the evolution of an owl that hoots back in the trees with the coming of sundown. Men search and research, offer theories, and make discoveries about their planet that are as exciting as any being made about the moon and other planets. And for the dreamer as well as for the scientist, the Grand Canyon has its spell and mood of excitement, and in its totality draws admiration from the untrained as well as trained.

We watch the sunset at Point Sublime, see night engulf the temples before us, watch the stars appear in the firmament. This time the wind has died at sundown, and no noise but the owl's breaks the stillness.

On our way back we notice white splotches in the dark. Everything else is at rest for the night—the paintbrush, cactus, gilia, juniper, yucca—but the evening primrose has bloomed, a beacon to night-flying moths. A new community is coming to life. Bats can be seen in the darkening sky, and those small passageways through the grass and sagebrush are no doubt becoming occupied with the usual nocturnal traffic of rodents.

Night passes with silence and stars and the calls of an owl. Once a coyote's voice echoes along the rim.

At dawn we return to see if the primroses, delicate, pure, fragile, are still there. They are. In a few brief moments, perhaps an hour, they will fold and be gone.

But their brilliance, their delicacy, the marvelous fragile way they fit into the ecosystem, and the way that ecosystem fits into the adventurous process of wearing down a canyon—these are worth the ruts, the rocks, the high centers, the scratches, the curves and dust of the road to Point Sublime.

We came back to the north rim village one evening, after a trip to Point Sublime; we were laden with dust, browned by the sun and wind, tired but refreshed and exhilarated. We pulled up to the lodge; it was a familiar, and even pleasant, sight—the lobby, the open terrace, the dining room, the curio shops. We had seen it many times before. But now it impressed us as being incongruous here.

After the sound of wind in the pines, the glitter of aspen leaves as they rustled in the sun, the music of thrushes, the silence of cool green vales, this collection of man's works seemed unduly intrusive.

Why it had not been built away from the rim, or even out of the park entirely, was understandable. In 1928, when Grand Canyon Lodge was completed, tourism being a critical matter, the custom was to locate public dining and sleeping quarters as near as possible to points of interest. Today, an unspoiled canyon rim is much harder to find than a lodge. A national park has come to be valued for fresh breezes rather than air brakes, the songs of birds instead of the ring-ing of telephones, the homes of squirrels, not of men.

We can find men and telephones and air brakes elsewhere for there is no shortage of them. But fresh breezes and bird songs and squirrel homes are no longer as commonplace as they used to be. Delicately balanced natural environments have become very rare indeed, and it struck us that here, where everything was supposed to be natural, where a "spell" of the primeval was supposed to prevail, nothing should interfere with the network of ecological relationships. This rim, unsullied for a hundred miles, was unique. It should have re-mained that way.

The Canyon, it seemed to us, had not been made to receive large human dwellings. In a way they seemed to break the spell. The rim had its own design, which could not be matched by artifice. Man could harmonize and blend his structures with nature, to be sure, but when we recalled the graceful forms of pinnacles and ledges, the gently curving slopes, the flowing design of the forest spilling into the Canyon, it seemed that here for once man should have denied himself the power to disturb, to dilute, and to pollute the spell.

In a few places along the rim we could see walls lined with fossils of creatures that lived some 200 million years ago, walls embedded with life left behind with the retreat of ancient seas. The rim had since been carved by eons of rain and flood.

As we came back from Point Sublime we preferred to think that man's most noble service had been to try to preserve this scenic masterpiece. From our winter's day at Cheyava Falls to this one on the old dirt road to Point Sublime we had learned to see the gorge not as separate pieces but as a whole. The loveliness of it, we saw, was not to be experienced in a hurried view from a man-made ter-race, but rather in the enjoyment of a web of wonder that surrounded the entire Canyon.

99

8

LONESOME VALLEY

OUR GUIDE to Toroweap was Captain Dutton. Although his information came to us across the span of a century, his insights and observations were still valid. In places this stable, wide-open land has changed very little in a hundred years.

Even in Dutton's day the route as far as Pipe Spring was easy and well-traveled. We covered in a few minutes what must have been an hour's ride for him. In his day, the Mormon fort at Pipe Spring, just inside the Arizona boundary, was less than a decade old, but had become a landmark even then, its sandstone walls providing shelter from marauding Navajos and Paiutes, its copious spring a source of water for livestock that roamed the range abundantly. The first telegraph line to the Territory of Arizona had been strung to the fort just a few years before.

Dutton learned that the land around the fort had once been thick with grass, but he could scarcely find a blade of it within ten miles. He attributed its absence to the general aridity of the region and to the foraging by cattle before seeds had ripened and fallen for next year's crop.

The road from Fredonia still crosses flats of sparse vegetation, stirred up by tall dust devils that look like slender brown tornadoes. Blank, Dutton called it, lifeless, expressionless as the sea.

We had traveled north from the north rim, down the Kaibab slope to Fredonia and west. The Vermilion Cliffs that rose behind Pipe Spring (the fort is now preserved as a national monument) endowed this region with a wealth of pastel hues that somehow

Tonto Platform, near the mouth of Toroweap Valley.

mitigated the cruelties of the desert. Though neither blank nor life-less, still the vegetation was simply snakeweed, sagebrush, and tum-bleweed, high contrast to the spruce-fir forest of the Kaibab.

We turned off the main road and drove past the warning sign: *Unimproved Road. No gas, oil, water or lodging. Grand Canyon National Monument 57 miles.* Just beyond, a dancing dust devil crossed our path, its tubelike column of wind and heat and dust curving and twisting like a waterspout.

The road aimed toward Mount Trumbull, black and flat-topped, visible forty miles ahead. We moved along rapidly, grateful for the road, rough and dusty as it was. We did not have a problem of water shortage, which the early geologists had. Only so long as their water held out, could they endure the temperature, which they compared to that of a furnace.

The sunflower seemed to Dutton the only flower that flourished in all the heat. We passed masses of prickly poppy, then crossed Bulrush Wash. Tamarix lined the washes, and tumbleweeds, another exotic, gathered against the banks. Shrub lines of Apache plume marched along the river terraces.

Sometimes the road stretched out straight ahead, shimmering in the morning heat, which had risen to only about 100 degrees so far. Sometimes we came to sudden dips, the bottoms of which we dared not judge until we were in them. In certain spots the road became narrow. In others we plowed through puddles of what could only be defined as liquid dust; it splashed high into the air, engulfed the car, and seeped into every corner, every pack, every sleeping bag, and into eyes, ears, noses, clothes. Dust may have bothered the early explorers in lesser amounts if they traveled where the route was grassy, but they still had a certain amount of it to contend with.

Dust devils danced on the plain again. The farther we went, the higher the yellow sandstone cliffs became. Platy shale or sandy ledges had broken off to form tumbled tablets along the slopes of gentle hills, and to the southeast more cinder cones appeared.

Flocks of horned larks flew up at our approach. Ravens lifted their shining black wings and rose into the air. A dry-land flora, consisting principally of cactus and yellow composites, grew among the lime-stone blocks. A richer variety thrived in moist places along the few intermittent streams we passed.

Dutton and his crew depended constantly on these stream beds, some of which had pools that retained water long after rains had passed and surface waters ceased to run. In these water pockets they filled their kegs from time to time and were able to continue indefinitely through what they called the outspreading desert—"which is not without charms, however repulsive in most respects." Dutton's advantage was that he knew which shales yielded fine impervious clays, excellent for puddling water in holes and basins.

Up a steep slope, through a narrow cleft in the ridge, and we came out on a grassy juniper upland. We had risen again to 6,000 feet, and the land lay covered with sagebrush, globemallow, paintbrush, and cactus with pink and yellow flowers.

We had gone thirty miles without evidence of human habitation, or at least little more than fences, roads, and abandoned corrals. No electric lines connected this land with the outside world, a matter that might concern those persons charged with rural electrification; but perhaps it is just as well to some of the residents, who may have their own generators. We saw no channels of communication, no unsightly telephone poles and wires. Whatever goes long distance here is sent by air or is carried.

Suddenly the red, sandy soil of the roadbed ended, and cinders began. We had entered volcanic country. Mount Trumbull, with its associated peaks and cinder cones, spread out ahead like black dunes mantled in forest green. "Their tumultuous profiles and gloomy shades," Dutton wrote, "form a strong contrast with the rectilinear outlines and vivid colors of the region roundabout."

In time we came to the head of Toroweap Valley, which began as a gentle depression, one of many in the Arizona Strip. *Weap*, a Paiute word, means "wash" or "valley," and *toro*, as near as can be told, refers to greasewood, a plant of the genus *Sarcobatus*.

But sagebrush rather than greasewood dominated the scene as the route dropped down from juniper country and into the valley itself. The only interruptions in the vegetation were ant mounds that covered wide circles of ground.

The walls began to rise on either side, though the valley retained its broad and gentle contours. Along the western rim Mount Trumbull took command. Both sides of the valley became enclosed with white, cream-colored, tan, and ocher cliffs that seemed to Dutton profiles of wonderful grace and nobility. He wrote:

103

As we put miles behind us, we find the banks on either side rising in height, becoming steeper, and at last displaying rocky ledges. In the course of six or seven miles the left side has become a wall 700 feet

Sunset over Toroweap Valley.

high, while the other side, somewhat lower, is much broken and craggy. Huge piles of basalt lie upon the mesa beyond, sheet upon sheet, culminating in a cluster of large cones. . . .

In the background the vista terminates at a mighty palisade, stretching directly across the axis of vision. Though more than 20 miles distant it reveals to us suggestions of grandeur which awaken feelings of awe. We know instinctively that it is a portion of the wall of the Grand Cañon.

Dutton took a day to ride down the valley, and in so doing saw a great deal more than modern travelers who cover the distance in less than an hour.

Above him unusual pinnacles in many shapes and sizes had weathered out of the Kaibab limestone. The fancy is kindled as the eye wanders over them, Dutton said, and he compared the strange profiles, the alcoves, the pediments, decorations, "statues" and "friezes" to the architecture of the Thebaid or of the Acropolis.

That has not changed. The great resource of this valley—its ability to stretch the vision, to draw interesting images from man's imagination, to overshadow familiar and less inspiring sights—remains as it was in the days of the early geologists. The valley, still reasonably wild and unscarred, has not had its walls or rims disturbed by the works of men. No one has installed a lodge and cabin here, or tried to blend a church into the background, and the singular effect is that the work of creation is displayed in a positive, unsullied manner.

Our eyes were not drawn to one type of architecture which one architect designed and other men built. Here we had the freedom to observe a line of natural forms, built of materials men cannot duplicate.

No matter how pleasing his architecture and skillful his design, or how brilliant his engineering, man's monuments are not appropriate here. In this place nature has sculpted a garden of statues and pinnacles, embossed them with raised designs, and set them on a gentle rise beneath a clear blue sky. Such a work needs no more retouching than does the statue of David. It can receive additions and subtractions only by nature itself, as only Da Vinci could alter the Mona Lisa.

A week would not have been enough to explore the walls of Toroweap Valley or the lava flows and caves and forests upon and beyond its rims.

Where lava poured into the Grand Canyon.

A lifetime would scarcely reveal all that there is to see in the Toroweap portion of the Grand Canyon, which was established as a national monument by presidential proclamation in 1932. Its nearly 200,000 acres contain more diversity than perhaps any area of equal size in the Canyon region.

The lava is its principal feature and reason for being. Sandstone cliffs and adjacent rocks are closely similar to those in the rest of the Canyon, but here about a million years ago—very young in the geologic sequence of events—great quantities of lava poured out.

Around the mouth of Toroweap Valley, where Toroweap Creek, if there were one, would have joined the Colorado River, lava erupted from more than sixty volcanic craters spread out toward the west and northwest of the junction.

Molten material flowed forth in what spectacles we know not. Very likely they had a little of the drama of present-day fountains, flows, and explosions of Hawaiian volcanoes.

It was not an unusual event. Volcanoes are common on the Colorado Plateau, of which some 15,000 square miles have been covered by eruptive igneous rocks. But here some of the lava flowed over the edge of the Grand Canyon, plunged down the sheer walls into a gorge 3,000 feet deep, and dammed the Colorado River.

As the Pine Mountains built up, they sent one flow after another down to the river, with the result that the Colorado was blocked by a dam nearly 500 feet high.

We can imagine steaming, smoking, incandescent flows pulsing down Toroweap Valley, searing the vegetation, burning the prairie, filling the clear desert air with a pall of smoke, then easing over the edge of the red-walled rim.

On plunging into the river, or into the lake that formed behind the dam, they must have sent up clouds of steam, as when Hawaiian lavas pour into the sea. One fluid and fiery flow followed the Colorado River for more than eighty-four miles downstream.

"What a conflict of water and fire there must have been here!" wrote John Wesley Powell on his pioneer river trip. "Just imagine a river of molten rock running down into a river of melted snow. What a seething and boiling of the waters; what clouds of steam rolled into the heavens!"

A cone erupted less than a mile from the rim itself, a cone that Dutton later named, most aptly, Vulcan's Throne.

Colorado River gorge from Toroweap overlook.

The final result of all this igneous action does indeed look like a kingdom of Vulcan. The smoke and steam are gone. The incandescence has flickered and died. Volcanic craters in the Pine Mountains are covered with conifers and sagebrush, and the Hell Hole, a nearly closed basin of red and white sedimentary strata, lies steeply pitching and wearing away. Mount Trumbull, edged with basaltic cliffs more than 100 feet high, is covered with conifers as well as a few bright patches of aspen. Eastward across the Kanab Plateau, a black lava flow at the head of Tuckup Canyon looks incongruous against the background of brightly colored sedimentary outcrops.

Remnants of the old lava dam may still be found, though the Colorado River, in breaching and wearing it away, is now down fifty feet below the base of the original dam. A curious lava monument, fifty feet high, still remains in the middle of the river.

The record also lingers upstream, high on the walls of the present canyon. Water-borne gravels lie perched in alcoves well above current river level, and mud and debris deposited on old shore lines of the ancient reservoir still cling to the cliffs.

Such is the essential aspect that inspired the proclamation of the national monument, but lava is by no means the only asset of this westward extension of the Canyon region. Part of it overlooks Kanab Canyon, which joins the Colorado River from the north. Kanab Creek gorge may well be one of the narrowest, steepest, deepest in the Canyon complex. At its lower end the creek, which has cut into a handsome red esplanade, must have scarcely an hour or two of direct sunshine a day, and in places none, somewhat reminiscent of the Little Colorado River as it joins the Grand Canyon farther east.

The Toroweap country has other extraordinary views: great pinnacled promontories, domes and cliffs, the butte of Mount Sinyala, a natural arch in Fern Glen Canyon, springs here and there. The scene at the lava site is as sheer as any in the canyon. The cliffs fall away 3,000 feet at a point where the main gorge is less than a mile in width. Ruins of prehistoric Indians abound throughout the area; at least 150 are known.

And as in all the remote corners of the Grand Canyon, this part possesses the wonders of solitude. District Ranger John Riffey, a tall and distinguished man-of-all-trades, had been in charge for more than twenty-eight years at the time of our visit. There must be something unusually compelling about a place that keeps him among what others consider hardship, dearth, and privation.

We talked with him a long time but never asked whether he got lonely. It would have been a foolish question. If "lonely" were meant in the sense of "desolate," "abandoned," and therefore "unhappy," nothing could be farther from the kind of existence John and his accomplished wife, an ornithologist, lead.

If "lonely" meant away from the bustle and noise of urban activity, then John would probably have replied that he was lonely and mighty glad of it.

Visitors to this out-of-the-way place number some fifteen hundred per year. Most know exactly what they are getting into because they have obtained information about the area in advance. Once in a great while comes a person who missed the signs and thought he was traveling to the north rim of the Grand Canyon, high on the Kaibab Plateau. He has come on and on, beaten up his car unexpectedly, and gotten covered with dust and perspiration. He is hungry. The car is low on gas. When he arrives at the ranger station John Riffey must explain to him that he missed a turn somewhere, must go back more or less the same way he came in, and has still 140 miles to go before he arrives at the north rim.

John's job is thus that of a diplomat, advising the newcomer that this remote area has no food, water, or lodging. John can do it. He can even persuade the visitor to finish the final winding five miles of road to take a look at the view from Toroweap Point before starting on the long trip back. John will give him a drink of water before sending him out into the heat, but fortunately doesn't have to do that very often. His own supply comes from a sixty-by-ninety-foot water-catchment basin near his house, which usually supplies all he needs; a rainfall of one-tenth inch gives him about three hundred gallons of water. Only once has he had to haul water, and that was when the annual rainfall did not exceed five inches.

If the visitor is about to run out of gas, John will direct him to a ranch some miles back up the road where a limited supply may sometimes be purchased.

Occasionally a visitor refuses to accept the blame for having taken a wrong turn. The wrath of heaven then falls on state and Federal agencies for not having signed the junction properly, not having improved the road, not having facilities to take care of the public, and so on. One man resolutely insisted that he was going to leave the area by some road other than the one he had come in on.

But these are exceptions and extremes. The average visitor appreciates the loneliness and solitude of Toroweap country. He revels in it. He knows that the long route of access will insulate him against the familiar noisy crowds that take away the silence of other places.

Even without visitors, John Riffey is, in a sense, neither alone nor isolated.

Pronghorns wander across the prairie of Toroweap Valley just below his house, and he is trying to increase their population, which was much larger before the advent of white men.

There is always the song of Scott's oriole to keep him company, and it is doubtful that he ever misses the music of civilization, what with the songs of canyon wrens echoing down from the crags above. Every day he can expect to be serenaded by a pack of coyotes, whose music interrupts the stillness of the evening, begins with a long sirenlike wail, then diffuses into short yips, and becomes a whole chorus. These are the wild voices of which a man like John Riffey could never grow tired.

Once in a while he sees the pink Grand Canyon rattlesnake, or the pygmy or the black-tailed rattlers. Lizards are his neighbors. His garden is nature's, stretching from rim to rim, where yuccas explode in a shower of white blooms every spring, and beargrass (not a grass but a member of the lily family) lifts a stalk of yellow flowers in June.

Because he has been there, because the law of the land requires that he keep the area undisturbed, other lovers of the wilderness can share some of his experiences. After a few days of wandering over the trails, climbing the cinder cones, scanning the ledges, or just sitting beneath a juniper tree and contemplating an alcove in the greatest cathedral on earth, a man's outlook and alertness may be considerably improved.

And you say to yourself at such times, let there be one road that is tough to travel, one section of this region that is difficult to reach. Let there be at least one unimproved place for the young and old to test their self-reliance. Let there be one of Dutton's domains preserved the way it was when he came.

Once you have heard the voice of Say's phoebe or the coyote or the canyon wren, you will realize that you did not plan enough time to stay, and you will depart with the same feeling Dutton had when he wrote:

"We leave the Toroweap Valley and the Grand Cañon, regretting that all its wonderful and instructive subjects should receive such brief notice."

Yuccas bloom on a red-rock esplanade at Toroweap.

9

INNER CANYON

NINETEEN TRAILS, and probably more, reach into the Grand Canyon from its rims. The early Indians had their own special routes, possibly along trails pioneered by wild animals, and sometimes present-day hikers still come across well-worn trails that have been preserved in the dry climate and may not have been trodden by man for eight hundred years.

Hiking is only one method of entering the Canyon. It may well be regarded as the safest, but the fact is that certain trails are distinctly unsafe.

Most reach from the rim to the river, and some join lateral trails such as that to Clear Creek. All this amounts to a kind of network, and it is possible to spend weeks hiking in the Canyon without retracing a great many steps.

However, some knowledge in advance about these trails is considered essential for mastery by the untrained. And a great deal of preparation is required before taking off on a long trip into some of the most severe hiking environments in North America.

"It is a very unfriendly environment for hiking," the chief ranger once told us, "especially in summer, when the greatest volume of hiking occurs."

Inner-canyon trails have taken the lives of many hikers. If there was ever a place where men can test the limits of their endurance and self-reliance, it is within this Canyon. Heat, thirst, hunger, danger, isolation, and disaster become the unwanted partners of the unprepared. But they are also part of the adventure, and if properly

Boulders beside the Colorado River, near the mouth of Ruby Canyon.

prepared, hikers may enjoy some unparalleled experiences within this Canyon.

The most popular trail is Bright Angel Trail, which zigzags down slopes along the Bright Angel Fault near Grand Canyon Village. For a distance of eight miles hikers descend from one amphitheater into another, passing the oasis of Indian Gardens halfway down (the last sure source of drinking water) and proceeding into the inner recesses of granite walls that border the Colorado River.

The trail is wide and well maintained, rarely if ever frightening hikers by closely bordering abyssal drop offs. Water is available at various points along it, and Indian Gardens is the main source of supply for Grand Canyon Village. Pumps at that point send water up 3,100 feet vertically where it is stored in tanks on the rim. Telephones are also available along the trail in case of emergency, though rescue is an expensive proposition; any hiker who becomes what is known as a drag-out—that is, someone who must be carried out by a mule sent to any point along the trail—pays a fee of twenty-five dollars or more for mule and guide.

The hazard is that inexperienced hikers, joyous over the ease of descent, enrapt by the amphitheater that surrounds them, forget that they must hike back up at the end of their trip. The turnaround comes after they have already expended a great deal of energy, and the hardest part is then ahead of them. Worse yet, at this elevation of nearly 7,000 feet, any expenditure of energy places an added strain on heart and lungs. Persons unaccustomed to high altitude will find themselves panting vigorously on the way uphill.

One scenic disadvantage of the Bright Angel Trail is that it offers few wide views of the canyon. The Kaibab Trail, on the other hand, especially its southern section, traverses a ridge from which extraordinary views may be had upstream and down. The Kaibab Trail, a cross-canyon route of twenty-one miles, connects Bright Angel Point on the north rim with Yaki Point on the south rim.

From Yaki Point hikers—who must start well equipped with water, for none is available on this trail—descend steeply along ridges and over jutting promontories until they reach the river 6.5 miles later.

The foot of this trail and the foot of the Bright Angel Trail are linked by a 1.8-mile route that winds along cliffs overlooking the sometimes turbulent, sometimes placid Colorado River. In a few places the trail affords access to boulder-strewn sand banks along the river.

Since these trails are regularly maintained by the National Park

Service, they provide excellent circular hikes for persons wishing to enter the Canyon. The trails are sometimes damaged; summer cloudbursts dig out sections or cause steep slopes to slump across the path. Crews set to work repairing the damage as soon as they can get there.

Once in a millennium comes a flood so devastating that whole sections of trail are washed away. This happened in 1966 along the north section of the Kaibab Trail. Great walls of water roared down Bright Angel Canyon (and down Clear Creek and other canyons as well), tore out vegetation, uprooted giant cottonwoods, washed away mud and gravel deposits that were centuries old, sheared off cliffs, and spread debris in as massive and sudden a relocation program as nature offers in this canyon. Under such circumstances, trail damage may be so extensive as to require several years for repair.

Most trails within the Grand Canyon (described in Appendix 1, pages 208–211) were pioneered by animals, Indians, and explorers, and later improved by citizens of communities within the Canyon region. Most were built before establishment of Grand Canyon National Park in 1919. The main routes have been improved by the National Park Service, but the rest have been abandoned and allowed to crumble and decay.

Some of the reasons for this are budgetary; it costs $1,000 a mile a year to keep each Canyon trail in shape. Another reason is lack of demand, although today the use of abandoned trails is increasing rapidly (a permit is required to hike on non-maintained trails). Some people question whether these trails should ever be improved, reasoning that they are part of an era of Canyon exploitation that is better forgotten. Other persons see no harm in maintaining them in a more or less primitive condition, as though to preserve their historic value and thus recall an era of exploitation we should not repeat.

The prevailing opinion trends toward leaving them as wilderness trails, without improvements, without signs, without facilities of any sort, and with only the barest maintenance, if any. That way hikers must use considerable ingenuity to find their way.

Some portions of trails have been obliterated by slides, and hikers must step with care across these sections: a few rocks may be ready to roll. On the other side hikers face the bewildering prospect of trying to find the trail again. Cross-country travel between sections of trail is not uncommon, but hikers may have to crawl on hands and knees to negotiate difficult cliffs. In a few places trails are vague, marked only by crude rock cairns if at all.

117

Some trails are pretty far gone. A National Park Service booklet issued to prospective hikers says that the Hance Trail, "or what remains of it, is characterized by an inability to see what lies ahead, total disappearance of the way every few hundred feet, and a seemingly illogical route of travel. The trail veers to the right, doubles around corners, and plunges abruptly downward in the most unexpected places. Throughout this erratic course, the route nevertheless touches certain key points which must be attained if the hiker is to continue. Those who cannot stay with the route will only compound their difficulty by proceeding further."

Confusion is not uncommon. Trails made by feral burros mingle with man-made trails. During the descent of an old steep route hikers may easily pick out the twists and turns of the trail below; but when they try to come back up, the trail is much more difficult to see, and they may thus have trouble fixing their direction of travel.

Yet for all the troubles, there is little question that the discoveries to be made within this Canyon are worth the efforts required to get down. Aridity and barrenness, as seen from the rim, are deceiving. Within those red walls exist innumerable little worlds, surprising worlds, and hundreds of hidden paradises, as well as extremely complex ecosystems as fragile and interesting as those on the rim.

Equipment for a one-day hike need not be elaborate. Usually a person cannot travel very far and still return the same day; hiking is much slower on the upgrade. Nevertheless, certain decisions must be made in advance, and a great deal depends upon personal preference.

As for clothing, it is always a good idea to take some sort of a hat. One does not need a sun helmet because a lightweight floppy hat that falls down over the ears is lighter, less expensive, and can be stuffed into a back pocket when not in use. Something should cover the neck. Sunburn and sunstroke are serious dangers on the Colorado Plateau. Ordinarily the air is so free of particles that the sun's rays pass through the atmosphere with little interference and burn the human skin most readily. Therefore we always carry a large bandanna to tie around the neck during the hottest part of the day.

Likewise, a long-sleeved cotton shirt seems to us to be essential. One can, of course, hike naked; some years ago a hiker walked the canyon from end to end wearing only boots and pack much of the way. Granted these degrees of freedom, the point about a long-

Where delicate plants may fail, the mustards root and thrive.

sleeved shirt is that when the hiker has had an overdose of solar radiation, he can put on the shirt and roll down the sleeves. It is no fun to be baked in the bottom of the Grand Canyon. Anyone who has tried to wear a hiking pack after a careless day in the sun will know the meaning of these words.

Travelers exceedingly sensitive to solar radiation need not deny themselves a trip into the Canyon, but they may have to take special precautions—as for example lightweight gloves to prevent burns on the hands. Each hiker should have some idea of his endurance quotient—and his burning quotient—in the wild. The motto here is: Expect a burning sun and prepare accordingly.

We have always felt, for specific reasons, that the lower part of the body should be well protected. Much depends upon what each hiker intends to do, but we think that long trousers and high boots should be the order of the day. We usually carry lightweight, low, soft shoes in the pack, and occasionally wear them on the trail, but our preference is for boots because we often leave the trail (hikers must have a permit to leave the trail) to explore a hidden canyon, pursue some animal, photograph a flower, or otherwise get involved with nature. Trousers and boots give some (but by no means total) protection against piercing cactus spines and projecting corners of rocks.

Good boots give the hiker some security with regard to rattlesnakes, too, though he seldom encounters any. There may be less chance of turning an ankle if the ankles are well supported, something to remember in rough terrain. Without having to give such close attention to where he steps, the hiker can make a bit more rapid progress and see more of the wonders around him.

The boots should be well-fitting. Socks should be sufficiently resilient and well-made that they will not bunch up, slide, or wear out too rapidly; any hiker who is uncertain about this should take some preliminary hikes and test the kinds of socks he prefers. Wool socks, reinforced with nylon for durability, have proved reliable.

120

These are not universal laws; they vary with each individual's experience. We have settled upon them only after years of hiking in the plateau country.

In pockets we carry knife, notebook, handkerchief, and hand lens for close examination of flowers, rocks, and minerals. Around the neck go binoculars and camera. These days, tiny tape recorders with such superb fidelity are available that we have added one to our gear; bringing back some of the inner-canyon music and song is often as thrilling as bringing back photographs. The sounds recapture living moments amid a wild orchestration of thunderstorms, waterfalls, wind, river, and animal notes and calls.

We have learned over the years to carry good quality packs with comfortable shoulder pads, readily available in sporting-goods shops. In one or the other at all times, ready for any spur-of-the-moment trip, are three deerskin bags. One contains medical items: first-aid kit with extra bandages, snake-bite kit, triangular bandage, stick for chapped lips, sunburn lotion, and antiseptic salve. This bag weighs less than a pound.

The second one holds such sundries as extra handkerchief, paper or plastic cup, signal mirror, safety wood matches in waterproof foil strip, salt, soap, toilet paper, and can opener, all of which also weighs less than a pound.

In the third bag we keep a variety of foods for emergency use only, allowing for the possibility that we could be detained unexpectedly for a couple of days. With modern compressed, dehydrated, and freeze-dried foods, it is possible to get the equivalent of an entire beefsteak into a three-ounce package, a bag of apples into a tiny packet, a generous serving of cooked, ground chicken meat into a two-ounce envelope, a quart of milk into three ounces of powder, and two western omelets into about two ounces.

We also carry a tin of pemmican, which is made of seedless raisins, peanuts, soy oil, dextrose, and dried apples. Our favorite dessert is canned and prebaked pecan cake roll, so rich that four ounces nearly fill two hungry hikers. All this emergency food weighs just over a pound per person.

Thus the items that could be classed as survival materials weigh around three pounds, and could prove to be the wisest three pounds ever packed. We have not been compelled to test them for survival except in the interior of the Amazon jungle; but just knowing that they are there relieves the mind.

Many other lightweight foods may be obtained. Jerky, or dried beef, has become quite popular and is widely available in the Southwest. Our oldtime favorite of dried peaches has almost priced itself out of the market, but there are dextrose tablets, trail cookies, raisins, and other items that can serve as trail snacks.

Complete and more elaborate meals are now packaged in canned or freeze-dried form and are so feather light that they have effectively reduced the problem of weight for modern hikers. There are orange, grapefruit, and pineapple juice crystals, as well as cans of

121

salad—tuna, ham, crabmeat, egg, shrimp, or chicken, with dressing—which weigh two to three ounces each and serve four or five people. Other powdered or freeze-dried items include instant applesauce, beef stew, hamburgers, spaghetti and meat balls, beef stroganoff, carrots, peas, and potatoes, rice with oriental herbs, hot-cake and syrup mixes, and a wide variety of drinks from milk shakes to pink lemonade.

Obviously hikers need to find their way to a spring or other source of water to prepare most of these foods, but such lightweight supplies constitute an easy-to-carry life support system in regions where little is available naturally for human consumption.

Every authority agrees that the item of number one importance in the Canyon, especially along abandoned trails, is water. Some of the springs and streams within the Canyon are perennial and dependable. Some are not, and even if all were, it is possible for a person to get delayed, be unable to reach a spring, and hence become exceedingly thirsty.

The summer rainy season brings on cloudbursts, and these leave gifts of water in pockets. Such pools are unreliable, though, in quantity and quality, and at best should be treated only as a bonus.

The trouble is that temperatures within this canyon climb very much higher than a hiker may expect. In the bottom they approach 120 degrees in the shade in summer, and when you consider that the trail and the walls of confined canyons reinforce this heat by reflecting it into your face, the effect is truly that of the interior of a furnace. Practically every vestige of humidity evaporates, and sometimes there is even a hot wind to make things drier and stir up dust.

With such accelerated desiccation, each active hiker needs one gallon of water each day. Thus gallon-canteens should be a part of the canyon hiker's equipment. If he is going to be gone two days or more, he ought to carry enough for the trip, or be assured of replenishing what he uses.

If water runs short, the hiker in trouble can consider proceeding at night, when the temperature is lower and he himself suffers less loss of moisture.

We have hiked out of the Grand Canyon in the middle of July both during the day and after midnight. The daytime trip was very hot indeed, and in both cases we lost a great deal of body fluid through perspiration. The nighttime trip, illuminated by starlight—which is entirely adequate on well-maintained trails—was less demanding.

Wise Canyon hikers know what not to carry and what not to do. They take no motorized vehicle, no pets, no guns—all prohibited by park regulations. They stand on the outer side of the trail when meeting a string of mules, or wherever the chief mule skinner asks them to stand. They never throw rocks, even from abandoned trails, lest they hit a hiker below; with the flood of people into the wilderness these days hikers can be anywhere.

They do not collect rocks, cut trees, or pick flowers without a permit from the park superintendent. They keep their litter and pack it out. If not, the trails will soon be lined with refuse and then equipped with refuse cans, at which point the wilderness evaporates.

Despite the problems, despite the intimate hazards, and even though the demands on human energy are enormous, going by foot is still the best way to travel the trails of the Grand Canyon. You can go at your own pace, stop when you wish, linger at will, hurry or loaf, and be completely at ease.

The moment you commit yourself to being engulfed within this Canyon, you enter another world, a dozen worlds, a hundred, past and present, wet and dry, vertical and horizontal.

Down the Kaibab Trail from Yaki Point, trail signs denote the various rock formations, and each is an entry into the uncounted worlds of geologic time. For example, the Kaibab limestone represents remains of limy, sandy deposits left after several advances and retreats of the sea. In those early shallows, shellfish, corals, and sponges lived, and today their fossils are frequently visible in ledges along the way. The very presence of coral suggests a tropical or subtropical environment, utterly different from the present climate of the region.

The antiquity of the rocks manifests itself even in this early stage of the descent, for the Kaibab limestone was deposited at the end of the Paleozoic Era, around 200 million years ago. Thus every layer of rock beneath the rim dates back to Paleozoic time or before and is therefore an early testimony to the history of the earth.

123

These layers are virtually textbook pages, illumined with fossil casts, molds, and imprints, illustrations of life that take us back to the dawn of biological existence on earth.

A short way down the initial switchbacks of the Kaibab Trail is a secret of a different sort. The raising of all this land from sea level up to 7,000 feet could not have been accomplished without at least some breaking and slipping here and there. The layers may look level, but most are cracked and displaced, offset from one another, and even bent or folded. Some fractures extend for miles across the plateau and go hundreds or thousands of feet deep. They coincide, intersect, parallel—in fact, a geologic map of the Grand Canyon region is crisscrossed with so many faults that it looks like the vein pattern in a hackberry leaf.

These crustal shifts and adjustments must have caused rock masses to scrape and grind against each other with terrible force. We seldom see evidence where one rock face gnashed against another, but here along the Kaibab Trail is one of those rare spots where so much heat and pressure were generated that the interfaces of the rocks became slickened. In fact, their geologic name is slickensides, and one look is enough to introduce us to the profound and fundamental release of terrestrial energy.

The Coconino sandstone, next down in the layered rock sequence traversed by switchbacks, also dates back to the Permian period of time. The cliff is pure sand, light yellow, cross-bedded, the kind of profile we might get by cutting a desert dune in half.

Obviously, then, the Coconino consists of sands deposited in a shifting, sweltering desert. It must have been an enormous desert; the formation covers an area of 32,000 square miles. It must have lasted a long time, too, because it varies in thickness from zero to a thousand feet.

By chipping along the surfaces of the ancient dunes (outside the park), familiar flagstone slabs, which cover many a patio and garden walk in the Southwest, can be extracted. Some of the slabs show tracks of ancient desert animals that skittered across the dunes: four-footed, lizardlike creatures, at least twenty-seven species of them in this and lower layers, with wide tread, narrow tread, long stride, short stride. Tracks are the only fossils; the animals that made them have not been found as yet.

The Kaibab Trail offers a great deal to look for, and hikers are free to stop wherever and whenever they please. Some sandy slabs deserve sustained inspection; certain pits are evidence of raindrops from a desert shower that didn't last very long. Such secrets were what we had wanted to stop and study on the trip to Cheyava Falls.

The mind is numbed by the antiquity of these rocks and the evidence of life they contain. Yet we are catapulted into an epoch even richer in life. Suddenly the rocks around us and the trail beneath us change from sandy yellow to dark maroon. The desert sands of the Coconino have abruptly given way to an accumulation of fine-grained sandy muds laid down on Permian stream banks. This is the Hermit shale. Red ripple marks, stopped by time and destiny, have come down through the millenniums displayed in artistic form.

Even more striking, a special "quarry," or place of excavation for scientific purposes, off to the side of the trail has been covered with glass to show the impressions of plants that grew on those ancient river banks. Thirty-five species are known from the Hermit shale, principally ferns and small cone-bearing plants, but there are also delicate insect wings and the footprints of salamanderlike creatures.

Both the Hermit shale and the 800-foot-thick Supai formation below it account for most of the red coloration of the Canyon. These hues come from compounds of iron—constituent of the muds and sands of ancient river banks and deltas. Short-legged, heavy-bodied animals, likely to have been amphibians, crawled across those muddy flats. Later deposits of mud or silt sealed their footprints, and erosion is just now revealing them once again.

Since this was before the age of the dinosaurs, and long before the coming of the great mammal era, the life was primitive indeed.

Like giant red stairsteps to nowhere, the prominent terraced slopes of the Supai formation lead to a sheer drop off—the Redwall limestone. We cross one final red rock terrace of blackbrush and Mormon tea, on which rise stalks of century plant, some twisted grotesquely. In the soil lie pieces of chert, a form of quartz, some red as jasper, some yellow, some brown—all fallen from layers of rock that once existed above and beyond.

Then the big cliff—and open space below.

We zigzag steeply down through gray marbled walls where the Redwall limestone displays its true color. Only in outward promontories, or wherever the Supai formation is missing above, does the Redwall reveal its typical gray. Elsewhere, its surface is coated with iron oxides washed down from the red beds overlying it.

Perhaps to most hikers there is little of interest along this portion of the trail, and they move rapidly on, getting dizzy with rapid turns in the trail. But those who pause can see embedded in the limestone, just at elbow height, millions of crinoid fragments, sections of ancient sea lilies that lived during the Mississippian period, 250 million years ago.

The Redwall limestone consists to a large degree of pure limestones, indicative of deposition at great depth in quiet seas. But some sections of it are made up almost wholly of the remains of corals, sea shells, and crinoids; examination under a hand lens reveals intri-

125

cate designs and elegant, living finery very old in the evolutionary structure of life.

Farther down in elevation and further back in time, a patch of lavender rock deposited during the Devonian period holds remnants of some of the world's first fish.

By the time we come to a ledge of Muav limestone we have reached the Cambrian period and returned to the very beginning of Paleozoic time. We have come back almost to the beginning of complex life forms, a time when worms and crablike trilobites crawled on the floor of the sea.

Across the open Tonto Platform we walk on Bright Angel shale, a greenish, micaceous stone, and have a little time to sort out the images that crossed our brains as we came down through so many ancient landscapes.

Time and life seem to blur. One image blends with another. But all is revealed in an orderly fashion, and if the human mind seems incapable of grasping the total significance at once, it is only as Captain Dutton said: knowledge of this Canyon and what it contains comes in slow successions and stages.

After many trips down that trail we began to grasp a few of the meanings. After repeated study we connected for ourselves the heights and depths, the relation of one formation to another, the succession of old life stages, and came to see how incomprehensible—though measurable—is the age of the Canyon.

Through a low pass in the Tapeats sandstone, a compaction of varied sedimentary strata rimming the inner gorge, we begin the steep and final descent to the river. In places we see great gaps in the geologic structure, where strata of one era rest directly upon the granites of an era twice removed. Half a billion years of earth history are lost in these gaps. Had any sediments been laid upon the land here then, the process of erosion wore them away before the Paleozoic deposition began.

126   Closer at hand we pass the Shinumo quartzite, a beautiful purple crystalline sandstone that has been so thoroughly compacted that its grains have fused into a solid mass.

Considering this and the handsome Hakatai shale just below, a striking reddish orange in the midday sun, we feel as though we were walking in some kind of a celestial mineral museum where the finest specimens have been set on display. The Hakatai, composed of muds that probably settled in shallow water, contains mud cracks and the molds of salt crystals but no life.

Indeed, we are so far down in the Canyon and so far back in time that there is little chance for life at all. The Bass limestone, lowest and earliest of the life-containing layers, has wavy lines that denote algal deposits from a reef so old that there may have been no animal life whatever, only pioneering microscopic plants.

Finally, in the Vishnu schist—black or dark green, flaky, mica-ceous—we come to the bottom of the Canyon and almost as close to the beginning of time as man is allowed to see. This formation is believed to be about two billion years old; whatever transpired before that is locked in the mystery of a planet's birth.

Great cliffs of granite and pegmatite, glittering pink and white in the sun, rise from the river's edge. So do cliffs of schist, sliced here and there with veins of quartz. Where streams have brought down sediments from side canyons, some of this rock has been smoothed over to exhibit superb cross-sections of highly contorted rock.

In the sometimes sharply curving lines or folds, the filling material of quartz, feldspar, and mica takes on an artistic quality. Small veins of red or pink, wide veins, long and short ones—all testify to the complex make-up of this rock and the seeming chaos of the inner gorge.

Winds have blown sand high along the bases of some of the cliffs, and chunks of schist and granite continue to fall down into the dunes. Loose sand along the river's edge is anchored by boulders or the roots of tumbleweed and catclaw. Here and there the roots of cat-claw have grown out through the dunes for many feet, and where the sand has been blown away from them, an intricate network of strands is exposed. In additional attempts to stabilize the slopes, nature has planted grass and cactus. The exotic Tamarix, or salt cedar, has also found its way here.

Thus barren as they look, and steep, and subject to severe extremes of temperature, these burning walls support a host of plants. Cactus, brittlebush, and Mormon tea are the principal species. We see an occasional agave. Catclaw does not limit itself to sands, but climbs up bouldery talus slopes. There are members of the composites, such as snakeweed, and many other forms. 127

Thus even the hottest, driest environment contains living organisms. So long as there is soil and perhaps a trifle of water, there will be life.

Captured within this hard-walled, rugged inner canyon, the Colorado River moves in an almost sullen fashion, like a caged beast shorn of freedom. For 1,440 miles it flows from origins in the Rocky

Mountains to endings in the Gulf of California. For a thousand of those miles it is trapped, cliff-bound and nearly inaccessible, receiving from occasional tributaries the soils of Wyoming, Colorado, Utah, and New Mexico before it reaches the Grand Canyon.

Though tamed in upstream reservoirs and its sedimentary load reduced, the river still gets muddy within the Canyon, still receives silt and boulders, still crashes against the pegmatite cliffs in its efforts to reduce the Canyon walls to a level plain.

Always above the hiss of rapids is the grating and grinding of the rocks beneath, rolling, cutting, and scouring. Always the river is in turmoil, its white and brown waters foaming, plunging and thrusting outward in repeating patterns.

"There are few operations of nature where the effect seems more disproportioned to the cause than in the comminution of rock in the channel of swift waters." So wrote George Perkins Marsh, the pioneering conservationist, in 1864. "Igneous rocks are generally so hard as to be wrought with great difficulty, and they bear the weight of enormous superstructures without yielding to the pressure; but to the torrent they are as wheat to the millstone."

The dams have not harnessed the spirit of the Colorado River. It still shows modern men a little of the ferocity it revealed to John Wesley Powell, and in some places is perhaps still as powerful and dangerous as it was in Powell's day.

On May 24, 1869, Powell embarked from Green River, Wyoming, with four boats and a crew of nine men, plus rations for ten months, and sextants, chronometers, barometers, thermometers, compasses, and other instruments for scientific examination.

He was no less than another Cook, another Flinders, another Franklin, who in earlier times had scientifically explored other parts of the world and whose accounts Powell might have read.

No one knew this river any more than Matthew Flinders knew Australia, or Sir John Franklin the Arctic. Powell intended to float down through the most mysterious of the canyons of the Colorado and right through the Grand Canyon itself. It was one of the most daring exploits of its time due to the awful dangers expected.

As great and veteran an explorer of the West as Captain John C. Frémont had little good to say of the river:

From many descriptions of trappers, it is probable that in its foaming course among its lofty precipices it presents many scenes of wild

The destiny of dust and sand is ultimately the sea.

grandeur; and though offering many temptations and often discussed, no trappers have been found bold enough to undertake a voyage which has so certain a prospect of fatal termination.

Powell himself considered the possibility that the expedition would come to a waterfall so great that it could not be passed, where the walls rose so sheer from the water's edge that the men would be unable to land and the water too swift to prevent their retreating upstream to safety. The only choice under those circumstances would be to run the falls, no matter how death-defying such acts would be.

The trip was indeed difficult, and by now is sufficiently well known that we do not need to go into detail here. Yet as a significant vector point in the history of the Canyon, it deserves some comment, for its relevance today and tomorrow has some interesting aspects.

"What shall we find?" he asked.

Day after day they floated down the river, skidding over sand-bars, coming to falls and rapids, and having to make one portage after another—it was fast going if they could make just thirty miles a day. Very often, as expected, the water completely occupied the channel. And frequently, too, the river roared in violence:

> Down the rapid river we glide, only making strokes enough with the oars to guide the boat. What a headlong ride it is! shooting past rocks and islands. I am soon filled with exhilaration only experienced before in riding a fleet horse over the outstretched prairie. One, two, three, four miles we go, rearing and plunging with the waves, until we wheel to the right into a beautiful park and land on an island, where we go into camp.

As the weeks went by the explorers passed and identified—or named—landmarks that have since become familiar along the river: Flaming Gorge, Canyon of Lodore, Split Mountain Canyon, Labyrinth Canyon, Music Temple, Glen Canyon. . . .

The group had its share of disasters and near-disasters: wrecks and rescues, oars lost, supplies and equipment tossed overboard, men catapulted into the water and nearly drowned, and instruments damaged.

"Everything is wet and spoiling," said Powell on one occasion. "The wind blows a hurricane," he said on another.

The voyage was a scientific one; yet Powell did his scientific work with intense personal pleasure:

> June 6. At daybreak I am awakened by a chorus of birds. It seems as if all the feathered songsters of the region have come to the old tree.

Several species of warblers, woodpeckers, and flickers above, meadow-larks in the grass, and wild geese in the river. I recline on my elbow and watch a lark near by, and then awaken my bedfellow, to listen to my Jenny Lind. A real morning concert for *me;* none of your "matinées!"

Nothing escaped his eye—the trees along the way, the appearance of aridity—"The landscape revels in sunshine"—a little of the wild-life, much of the Indian life, and a number of tributary canyons and rivers.

Clearly, he never ceased to enjoy the beauty and grandeur of the scene: "There is an exquisite charm in our ride to-day down this beautiful canyon." By July 4 they had been six weeks on the way, and by early August arrived in the Grand Canyon portion of the journey.

"Canyon walls, still higher and higher" . . .

"And now the scenery is on a grand scale" . . .

"Walls still higher; water swift again."

Three months, and conditions worsened; the men were plagued by rain and cold, sickness, despair. The boats leaked. Rations spoiled and had to be discarded. Some of the instruments were damaged. Constant portaging caused irritating delays.

But the drama of the scene was both inspiring and sobering:

We are three quarters of a mile in the depths of the earth, and the great river shrinks into insignificance as it dashes its angry waves against the walls and cliffs that rise to the world above; the waves are but puny ripples, and we but pigmies, running up and down the sands or lost among the boulders.

We have an unknown distance yet to run, an unknown river to ex-plore. What falls there are, we know not; what rocks beset the channel, we know not; what walls rise over the river, we know not. Ah, well! we may conjecture many things. The men talk as cheerfully as ever; jests are bandied about freely this morning; but to me the cheer is somber and the jests are ghastly.

Entering the rugged rocks of the inner gorge gave Powell mis-givings, for it was here that he expected to find the rapids at their highest and most hazardous. "We are in a granite prison," he said.

The rapids did thunder and roll, mightily and ponderously. The boats were small and unwieldy, ill designed for this kind of travel. So violent were some of the rapids that the boatmen had little con-trol—if any.

We hold, and let go, and pull, and lift, and ward—among rocks, around rocks, and over rocks. . . .

The waters reel and roll and boil, and we are scarcely able to determine where we can go. Now the boat is carried to the right, perhaps close to the wall; again, she is shot into the stream and, perhaps is dragged over to the other side, where, caught in a whirlpool, she spins about. We can neither land nor run as we please. The boats are entirely unmanageable; no order in their running can be preserved; now one, now another, is ahead, each crew laboring for its own preservation. In such a place we come to another rapid. Two of the boats run it perforce. One succeeds in landing, but there is no foothold by which to make a portage and she is pushed out again into the stream. The next minute a great reflex wave fills the open compartment; she is waterlogged, and drifts unmanageable. Breaker after breaker rolls over her and one capsizes her. The men are thrown out; but they cling to the boat, and she drifts down some distance alongside of us and we are able to catch her. She is soon bailed out and the men are aboard once more; but the oars are lost. . . .

One light in their "granite prison" was Bright Angel Creek, which Powell named. They explored it briefly, but haste became the order of the days, and they had to move on.

At times their passage was extremely good.

"Thirty-five miles today. Hurrah!"

"A few days like this and we are out of prison."

They came to the Toroweap area and its "great quantities of cooled lava."

Fears for safety of the expedition grew so great that three men decided to leave the party and hike out via the rim and overland back to some outpost of civilization. It was a painful separation, and as it happened, the three men who thus departed were never heard from again.

The rest of the party continued downriver, and by the end of August reached the end of the trip. In due course they went overland to Salt Lake City.

But there has been no end to the fascination which this daring gamble has kindled in the breasts of adventurous men since then. Powell went down the river again two years later, and for more than a century his trips have been repeated in one form or another by others. Boats have been modified; motorboats, rafts, and floats have been used. Two men even swam the river, from Lee's Ferry to Pierce's Ferry; but the river is so dangerous to swimmers that the National Park Service discourages this.

Winds along the river sort and sift the silt.

Those who have gone downriver speak of it with an air of casualness. "Well, of course," they say, "you haven't seen the Canyon until you go through it on the river."

Powell said much the same:

> You cannot see the Grand Canyon in one view, as if it were a changeless spectacle from which a curtain might be lifted, but to see it you have to toil from month to month through its labyrinths. It is a region more difficult to traverse than the Alps or the Himalayas, but if strength and courage are sufficient for the task, by a year's toil a concept of sublimity can be obtained never again to be equaled on the hither side of Paradise.

Those who float the river today seek something besides adventure, beauty, and isolation. There is a great deal more within the Canyon and along the river than is obvious from the rim. Much life abounds along what seems, from above, a barren river. On banks that receive large amounts of solar radiation, a desert vegetation prevails, adapted to extremes of heat and drought. A river runner glides past thickets of catclaw, often very dense. Among the boulders at the water's edge he sees saltbush, paintbrush, bee plant, datura, Mormon tea, squawbush, and single-leaf ash. Buckwheat and globemallow add touches of color to the boulder slopes, and prickly pear bears rich purple fruit on the talus slopes.

Panicum grasses decorate the dry sand. Here and there he sees a patch of willow hugging the edge of a cliff or individual willows venturing in a line along the river bank. Bur sage, kin to the ragweed, clings to dry corners. Brittlebush, browsed by bighorns, borders the dunes. In places one can see the graceful desert willow (actually a bignonia), whose lavender, white, and yellow flowers seem like orchids in this dry inferno.

All in all, a considerable living community occupies the river's edge and adjacent walls, much of it dependent on the Colorado River for water. Deer come down to drink. Bighorns wander across the ledges and sloping talus fields. Beavers inhabit the river banks, their numbers remaining in balance with available forage—the willows and cottonwoods they subsist on.

The river runner may also get a glimpse of rock squirrels, chipmunks, raccoons, amphibians, herons, egrets, ducks and geese in season, kingfishers, killdeer, sandpipers, avocets, doves, redwings, and others too numerous to mention.

134

Avocets at the edge of the Colorado River, near Bass Rapids.

Less dependent upon the river, but at home in the desert environment, are nocturnal animals such as bats (of which the Canyon has eleven species), pocket and cactus mice, kangaroo and wood rats, hawks, owls, and various reptiles.

Away from the river, too, are vales of paradise, sleepy hollows, and shady glens. When venturing up side canyons, the river runner comes upon cool refreshing streams and leaping springs, waterfalls in abundance, pools, seeps, and grassy meadows more common than suspected.

A typical one is Ribbon Falls, near Bright Angel Creek, about five miles north of the Colorado River. From a crooked, high-level spillway that obscures the Canyon just behind comes a bursting, outward-leaping, falling, spraying cataract of water so pure and sparkling it could be a tumbling carload of diamonds.

The sound of its gushing is magnified by the semicircular amphitheater into which it falls. Every tinkling note, every chime, every hiss echoes among the curving rims, reinforced by other notes that follow almost immediately. Together, they coalesce into a steady sound, but the fall is never so large that the ringing bells and chimes cannot be heard.

Some of the water sails into the air, some drips rapidly, some glides down a steep, green, mossy slope, some foams and sputters as it flows through vegetation.

By the time it reaches the bottom, the water has formed a glittering curtain of spray that surrounds a travertine cave. Within that curtain a visitor has the impression of being inside a shower of stars.

When the tired and dusty hiker, or river runner, soaked with perspiration, feels that water on his skin, the refreshing touch seems almost icy in comparison with his heated body. He knows no shower more welcome, but the water is cold, aerated in the shadows, fresh from some spring channel above.

There is in fact a multiplicity of channels through the Canyon rock layers. Water falling on the rims as snow soaks into the cracked and creviced Kaibab limestone, percolates downward, joins a reservoir of underground water and perhaps much later enters a canal that reaches the open air and plunges down a slope or cliff.

Cheyava Falls is that way. So is Thunder Spring, about fifteen miles west of Point Sublime, gushing out with a canyon-shaking roar; it plunges steeply into a ravine and, half a mile below, joins

136

In the inner gorge: the river as sculptor.

Tapeats Creek for a twisting, turning, tumbling, sliding three-mile journey during which it drops 500 feet in elevation to the silty Colorado.

Back in his boat after such excursions, the river runner can relax and rest and float along with his mind completely open. If rapids do not occupy him, his thoughts may drift as freely as a cottonwood leaf on the water. His only preoccupation is to watch the cliffs slide slowly by.

Or his gaze may become transfixed on the water, on the sand banks that occasionally line the river, on the sculptured grooves and scalloped grottoes where sediments scraping past have carved the walls, on the tumble of talus boulders where perhaps a lone bighorn is glimpsed, and on the endless friezes and bas-reliefs with which the cliffs have been ornamented by wind and rain.

He finds himself relaxed because there is no way to get wrought up. He knows that days later, perhaps years later, he can relive his experiences by walking to the rim and looking down. The adventures, the thrills, the scenes, the feelings will all leap to mind again. The world will stop for that precious moment. Action around him will freeze. Nothing else will be important just then. He will have crossed the threshold into another time.

For the moment, however, he absorbs the river's powers of renewal as fully as possible. When he has completed his trip, he will discover how much he has come to be in tune with nature, in tune with the silence and harmony of the route, and in tune with Powell, who said of the Canyon of Lodore:

"Its walls and cliffs, its peaks and crags, its amphitheaters and alcoves, tell a story of beauty and grandeur that I hear yet—and shall hear."

10

HAVASUPAI

THE DESCENT into Supai begins sharply. For 1,000 feet vertically the trail bends back and forth through light-colored cross-bedded sandstones, in and out of shadows, and over a long talus slope that gently leads to the floor of a sandy wash.

All about are rigid knee-high shrubs of blackbrush, a desert rose that may well cover more of the American Southwest than anything except the ubiquitous sagebrush, with which it often associates. In the Grand Canyon those low plateaus—the hot, dry, sunbaked slopes and platforms that spread out broadly and make up the floor and lower sides of the Canyon—often support so thick a cover of blackbrush that it takes on a grayish cast. The flowers of this shrub are not conspicuous—normally they haven't any petals—and it has little claim to fame. But for tenacity and durability the blackbrush commands respect, and for bighorns it may well be a staff of life: it withstands steady browsing by sheep and burros.

The going is easy. Over a wide floodplain that knows only excess waters of storm or melting snows of winter, the hiker turns almost due north, down Hualapai Canyon. His boots ring out as he passes over rock worn smooth by centuries of flood, or they grate in the gravel, or send a sandstone pebble singing.

Beargrass waves its giant plumes from the cliffs above; its stems may be two inches thick and the plumes a total of twelve feet high. The only touch of bright, rich green is that of single-leaf ash. Shrubs modify the desert milieu, breaking up the open places with their head-high thickets of mountain mahogany, oak, and squawbush. Junipers march at random in the draws, but Apache plume lines up in curving, well-dressed regiments.

The valley is wide, affording at first the fairest views of distant cliffs, the high Coconino with its sheer brown walls and yellow facades, and the sweeping talus over the Hermit shale.

Warning. Trail Subject to Flash Floods. This sign is to be respected, and a hiker must resolve to keep an eye on the sky—though spring is generally dry in southwestern deserts.

The path along the stream course descends almost unnoticed into a gentle swale. Red cliffs of the Supai formation rise on either side and loom ahead.

Before long the route becomes closed in by cliffs. The echoing click of boots on gravel returns from closer quarters and from small amphitheaters and semicircular alcoves. Giant red boulders rest in a sea of sand, their tips protruding like icebergs out of the ocean.

A hiker meets familiar friends with whom it is a joy to renew acquaintance. The stream bed has its share of seepwillow, which looks like a willow but is a composite instead, and heralds the presence of at least some moisture.

In wild-grape arbors we hear the calls of chats or towhees. A monarch butterfly passes by. A flash of red announces the gilia, a flash of blue the penstemon, of yellow the paperflower, of orange the mallow, of white the Jimson weed, of purple the aster. A bristly, tangled graythorn thicket borders upon the sand. The mesquites are in flower, and may continue to bloom into October. The general aridity of springtime makes little difference, or so it seems. Obviously, Hualapai Canyon is a botanical garden of rare good merit.

An hour passes. Shadows fill the steep declivity except where clefts above let in the sun. The defile narrows to a curving, red-walled corridor. Only occasional calls of canyon wrens interrupt the solitude—or better, magnify it.

Detached, released from cares, a hiker is completely unprepared for what he is about to see. He knows he is too far from the famous waterfalls of Havasu Creek to expect them around the coming bend. The trail remains too deeply embedded in stone to allow any scenic view.

140

The veil of repetition falls across his mind—the rhythm of footsteps, the ringing of gravel, the echoes among the alcoves—and lulls him into a mood that takes his thoughts away. He judges the Canyon here too dark and dry to support any masterpieces of botany. And on this latter point he couldn't be more wrong.

Havasu Creek, terraced by travertine, flows from pool to pool.

Rounding a bend in the trail toward a deep and darkened corner of the Canyon, he sees a flash of what seems like a green and purple fire exploding in the gloom. He cannot at first adjust his eye or mind to receive and register the sight, but he stops almost instinctively.

A shaft of sunlight, having picked its way through overhanging ledges, has succeeded in penetrating the darkness. By what appears to be extraordinary accident, it has struck a redbud tree as a spotlight touches a dancer.

The heart-shaped leaves have just begun their growth of spring, and the sun shines through them from behind. Never was a yellow-green more vivid, a contrast more intense. Not a breath of air stirs the newborn leaves. The green is an explosive green, yet it forms a bed in which the royal beauty of magenta may flourish. The tree is in full bloom.

Western redbuds, unlike their eastern counterparts, have flowers large in size and rich in reddish overtones. They seem to grow in denser clusters and fill the tree more fully.

The tree looks as though it had no limbs; it appears as a giant ball of green and violet, the flowers beginning to fade, the leaves coming on. The ball is lighted from within, bursting out in a display that equals the dazzling color and effect of fireworks. You can see a thousand blooming trees along a boulevard, but none exceeds the effect of this one, standing alone, unassisted by man, unmanicured, unclipped, unfertilized.

With awe and disbelief, the hiker advances slowly, lest the scene prove to be a dream which in a few more moments will disappear and never be regained.

But the "apparition" is real. It looms in size. As he walks beneath the tree magenta and green surround him, displacing the blue of the sky. Shadows vanish. Darkness disappears. He is enveloped in a world of infinite shape and overpowering color.

On close examination he sees that each leaf glows in several shades of green. Each has a network of veins arranged in palmate, fan-shaped form with scores of connecting canals. The closer he looks the more the miracle is magnified. Each blade has a different arrangement; he could not study them all or absorb the fullness of their beauty if he stayed there for the rest of the day.

Yet he is loath to leave. In one tree he has found a thousand sights and a thousand delights. They change. The flowers exhibit every

142

In the village of the Havasupai Indians.

shade of pink and lavender, depending on how the sun has caught them in a given moment. He would have to go to the Susitna River valley of Alaska, with its fireweed on the taiga, to find so elegant a display of green and lavender.

He turns once more before losing sight of it, turns and stares for a long moment. Vaguely he hears the call of the canyon wren, and that is a part of this experience, too. Human vanity and other driving forces of men lie a world apart. He has forgotten them.

This scene makes him conscious of a virtue that even Benjamin Franklin forgot. It gives him humility.

Pondering, lost in thought, step by step, mile after mile, he gradually drops into Supai. Suddenly, the long walk is over. A line of gleaming green cottonwoods indicates the presence of Havasu Creek, which rises out of the sand a few hundred yards upstream from the junction of Hualapai and Havasu Canyons.

Clear and cool, like the crystal water in a drinking glass, it is a major stream to begin with, flowing at more than sixty cubic feet per second and a temperature of seventy degrees. He feels the coolness and shade beneath the cottonwoods long before he reaches them. The fresh aroma of growth is welcome, for the noonday sun beats straight into the canyon, chasing out every shadow except for those beneath the overhang and cottonwoods.

The hiker dips his face in the clear water. He drinks and the energy of life seems to flow once more through his tired muscles. He rests, but not for long.

Up again and down the trail. A canal dug along the side of the creek is his first indication that this paradise is inhabited. A fence. A corral. A log lined with pack frames. A saddle. Brush huts. More fences. Apricot orchards. Fields of alfalfa. A store. A small lodge. A schoolhouse. Three-bedroom prefabricated houses. A tractor. Horses. Indian boys riding, laughing, kicking up the sand with their galloping steeds.

He has arrived at the home of the Havasupai Indians.

144

The canyon has widened. The line of cottonwoods along Havasu Creek swings off beneath the western wall; tall cottonwoods also grow throughout the valley. Above everything are two stone monoliths commanding the valley as though they were prince and princess. One hears various stories about them, for example, that they represent a boy and girl who sought a better life by climbing out of the canyon, and were turned to stone as an admonition to others that no better life exists outside.

Concerning the Havasupais themselves, it is hard to say when they entered this canyon and set up their comparatively idyllic existence. Evidence seems to suggest that early peoples moved into this area from the west before A.D. 600. Because of the canyon's natural resources, it may not have been abandoned during widespread drought, as happened elsewhere in the Southwest.

Nature favored Havasu Canyon with a sure and abundant supply of fresh water, a more than adequate growing season, and winters that seldom bring snow and indeed usually offer mild and sunny days.

The annual precipitation is only ten inches, but the Supais seldom had to cope with drought as did their Yuman cousins, the Hualapais, who occupy open arid lands beyond the rim.

The Havasupais numbered about 250 when first seen by Europeans in 1776, and their present population remains at a stable two hundred. Whether they are descended from the ancient Indians who occupied pueblo dwellings hidden here and there in the Canyon region is unknown, but there is some evidence for continuity.

Archeologists know that the region was previously occupied by a group of Indians who resembled the late Basketmaker and early Pueblo Indians. These people are called Cohonina, and since the Havasupais occupy an area previously inhabited by Cohonina, some archeologists believe that the Havasupais are descendants of those earlier people.

Today the Havasupais irrigate about three hundred acres, raising apricots, peaches, figs, melons, and squash. Land ownership is communal, and each family tends its own patches or fields. Corn is planted at intervals. So are beans. Peaches are dried and stored with other crops for winter use. The Indians gather wild foods such as mesquite beans, pinyon seeds, and cactus fruits; they go on rabbit hunts and seek what other meat they can, drying it in the sun.

They run horses above or below their village, wherever they can find the space. They also earn a supplemental income from tourists, who pay a fee for entering and a fee for photographing, and who may stay at the local hotel and purchase supplies form a tribal store.

The mail comes in from Peach Springs, to the south, but Havasu Canyon may also be reached from Grand Canyon Village via Topocoba Hilltop, a trip of thirty-five miles over rough dirt road and a pack-horse trip down fourteen miles of trail.

Thus the Havasupais are not entirely isolated; they have telephones and a post office. They depend considerably on catalogues to order what they want; crafts, such as basket-making, they rarely pursue any more.

The tribe has a chief and two subchiefs, but important decisions are made primarily through a tribal council, which is headed by a chairman and two vice-chairmen. The tribe is handling for itself such matters as economic development, law enforcement, and tribal administration.

The Havasupais ride hard and laugh uproariously, being among the most cheerful tribes we know. They have rodeos and races, some quite impromptu, and an August festival of the harvest. They have never been known to be warlike.

They also have hard times. Disastrous floods have ravaged their canyon, tearing out shelters, washing away fields, ripping up and relocating the stream bed of Havasu Creek.

Their biggest problem, ironically, is friendly outsiders. The Havasupais, like many another race on earth, have been condemned by white men for their customs and beliefs (their creation myths and other legends resemble those of Mojave and Yuma Indians), and persistent efforts have been made, with some success, to impose upon them alien practices and an alien religion.

Their manner of life—brush shelters, outdoor living, poor sanitation—have promoted cries of "poverty," and attempts to impose considerable change on the Havasupai way of doing things still continue. As in so many other countries, corrugated steel and quonset construction has been introduced where once were shelters of sticks and unique earth houses. Thus, many villages in the world seem to be moving toward a masking, self-effacing sameness. Such construction techniques do as much violence to Havasupai homes as to the village of Votualailai in the Fiji Islands, for example; yet each has fascinating original characteristics worthy of preservation.

Some outsiders deplore the notion that Supais have a life span of forty-four years. Something, they say, should be done about it. But what? Other people might reply that forty-four years of life in Havasu Canyon equal twice as many elsewhere.

The Havasupais have resisted a great deal of the change. Fortunate they are that no highways lead to their reservation yet and that their lands lie entirely within Grand Canyon National Park. That gives them a buffer, of sorts, against overzealous groups that threaten to

146

Havasupai Indian fields.

smother them with paternalism. If what they have be poverty, perhaps there should be more of it.

It is difficult to tell, from conflicting historic reports by persons untrained to appraise such matters, just how well or badly the Havasupais got along in their milieu before it was changed. Of all aboriginal tribes, they live in what may be regarded with a certain validity as the most beautiful environment anywhere. But more important is not, perhaps, how poor the people are but how well adapted to life in this canyon. Poverty, like everything else, is relative. A more realistic way of assessing the human condition might be to observe the adaptation of groups to their environment. What is "poverty" to one may be abundance to another.

In any case, it is to be hoped that the destiny of the Havasupais will remain to a considerable degree in their own hands, and perhaps, with "progress" approaching on all sides, they will have the wisdom to keep some of their canyon as it was. Perhaps even some of their original beliefs and religion can be perpetuated—if these have not been entirely expunged from memory.

The flood of tourists presents as serious a challenge here as elsewhere in the plateau country, and perhaps the Havasupais will some day limit the number of persons who can enter their reservation. Already their lovely stream has been polluted.

If there was ever a place that concentrates the enchantment of the plateau, it is this canyon. Down the trail a mile or so, the hiker re-enters the fresh riparian milieu of Havasu Creek. He is shaded by box elder, hackberry, willow, and cottonwood. Above, on the dry slopes, grow mesquite and catclaw. Where the finely powdered soil from floods in the past lies exposed to the sun, a network of brilliant magenta and yellow flowers nestles—the trailing four o'clock (Allionia).

Being a young stream, Havasu Creek is filled with cataracts, which can be heard roaring through the mesquites beyond the village. At the edges of pools grows watercress. Tangles of wild grape extend from barren cliffs to the side of the stream.

Soon the hiker comes to a spring and kneels to examine the microenvironment there: cool, wet, filled with sunshine, rich with maidenhair ferns, ablaze with red blossoms of mimulus, the monkeyflower—all with music of falling, flowing, and dripping water, which sounds

Curtains of travertine drape the amphitheater of Mooney Falls.

like tiny bells rushing down the mossy bank. Cruising overhead may be a sulfur butterfly or a mourning cloak, and in the trees a bright red tanager, possibly even a finch eating figs.

As an oasis in a desert of dry red rock, Havasu Canyon attracts many species of birds. The pools are visited by cormorants, grebes, and green-winged teals. Among the nesting species are coots, hummingbirds, and kingbirds. Water ouzels dip into and out of the water. Long-tailed chats sing and shout in the trees. Downy and ladder-backed woodpeckers shuttle between mesquites and cottonwoods.

The silent observer may expect to have a wood pewee for companion, or a black phoebe near the water. Flocks of blackbirds circle the fields, and for color, one may expect goldfinches and buntings.

Indeed, by staying awhile and creeping or sitting as quietly as the animals themselves, the hiker may see a great deal of Havasu Canyon's wildlife. Lizards abound, and some of them, like the collared lizard, are exceptionally colorful. King snakes occur, and so do rattlesnakes, which are seldom seen. In such an aquatic environment, frogs and toads find residence. In drier ecosystems jackrabbits, cottontails, ground squirrels, chipmunks, and perhaps a rare bighorn predominate.

Owing to a heavy concentration of calcium and magnesium carbonates, calcium sulfate, and magnesium chloride, the water of Havasu Creek coats everything it touches with travertine, which over the years has resulted in a mass of grotesque roots and molds of limbs and leaves; there are also stone draperies and stream terraces. Water gathers in limpid pools where refractions from bits of clay in suspension render it a turquoise blue. As a matter of fact, the canyon is named from this phenomenon: *haha* meaning "water" and *vasu* meaning "blue-green."

At the first sight of Navajo Falls, close to a hundred feet high, bursting through the shrubbery and over a mossy terrace, free-falling into a rich green pool below, a man may feel that he has found his Shangri-La. One terrace after another form a multitude of pools, and some of these the hiker crosses as the trail goes in and out of the woods.

Across a cactus meadow, he arrives at the boundary of the reservation and, re-entering Grand Canyon National Park, he steps down beside the wide white spray and turquoise pool of thundering Havasu Falls. The water looks inviting. He peels off his sweat-soaked

Havasu Creek near its confluence with the Colorado River.

garments and plunges in. The temperature, at 67 degrees, is cooler than he expected. The swim is a brisk one.

Exploring a side canyon here will reveal an old mine. A tunnel penetrates the Redwall limestone, and beneath the entrance, scattered about the tailings, are translucent crystals of calcite. The mine is abandoned now, but it recalls an era of the 1880's when efforts were made to extract the lead, silver, zinc, and vanadium locked in the limestones of Havasu Canyon. Those efforts had little success. The remoteness of the place protected it against overexploitation until the national park could be established.

Conversely, the canyon exacted its toll from the miners. One of them was an ex-sailor named James Mooney. Below Havasu Falls he came to a sheer cliff that extended from wall to wall, and if he wanted to get on down the canyon he had to descend that cliff. Havasu Creek plunges over the precipice in a waterfall some 200 feet high, but Mooney was more interested in minerals than scenery. He threw a rope over the edge and started down.

He never came back. Apparently the rope was too short. The Supais who were helping could not pull him back when the rope got caught, and were even unable to see him—or at least communicate details of the tragedy.

Mooney fell, and it was months before his body could be retrieved and buried on an island below the falls. That was in 1880. The grave has since washed out, but Mooney's name remains with the falls.

Today a safe but hair-raising series of steps, tunnels, and pegs enable the hiker to descend in a slower and healthier fashion than Mooney did. Once down, there is little question that the high green cottonwoods, crystal pools, grassy banks, rushes, wild celery, and orchids that line the stream render this cliff-walled vale one of the most beautiful in the Grand Canyon region. Thunder and spray overwhelm a visitor's senses and also refresh him. A bit farther down only whispering leaves and music from lesser falls stir the peaceful vales.

152 Down past the cascades of Beaver Falls the trail, or what there is of it, finally reaches the Colorado River, eight miles from the village. Here Havasu Creek meets the mighty river in languid emerald pools.

After this, the trip back to the village and then to the rim, whenever it is finally, reluctantly taken, becomes a montage of mingling sights and sounds. The music of falling water still rings in the hiker's ears. So does the laughter of Havasupai children.

Hiking out, with the cadence of boots on sandstone echoing among the canyon walls, he comes again to the redbud tree. Now it is in shade, subdued in color. No sun shines through the fresh green leaves or sets the lavender petals dancing with light.

Those earlier moments filled with light and color do not exist save in his mind, but the images have now been combined with scores of others. The green of the leaves merges with the emerald of pools. The purple flowers coalesce with purple cliffs that meet the light of dawn. He lowers his head and hikes on, yet knows that the shadows do not remain, nor the confusion of sights and sounds.

In the years to come, the rustling cottonwoods will lull him to sleep. The singing springs of Supai will recall to him the moments of perfection he encountered briefly. Thundering waterfalls will be remembered as vividly as waves on a tropic shore.

Happily, there are places still left in this land that must be earned—by hard work, by sweat, by perseverance. In this case the earnings are good, and the contentment of Havasu Canyon is contagious.

It has its problems; no place, no man, is without them. But when the hiker comes away, or perhaps when he just recalls that it exists, he remembers the goodness that exists on earth and realizes that some of it lies within himself.

And he is never quite the same again.

153

The multiple pools below Havasu Falls.

11

SUDDEN DANGERS

Ever since Europeans set foot in the Grand Canyon, men have attempted to take something from it, put something in it, or change it in one way or another.

The Spaniards wanted gold. Early American trailblazers looked for pelts of furbearers: James Ohio Pattie, Kit Carson, Jedediah Smith, Bill Williams, and William H. Ashley—all came to the Canyon with beaver in mind.

Beaver and dreams. For there was always the vague, unquenchable notion that a man might find some kind of Eldorado, some great cache of wealth, if not in gold, then in skins, and if not in skins, well . . .

Eventually, men came to survey trail routes, wagon routes, railroad routes. These expeditions, some of them military, brought such men as J. S. Newberry, a geologist who made the first scientific study of the Grand Canyon. Powell seemed led by a thirst for knowledge. "The exploration was not made for adventure," he wrote, "but purely for scientific purposes, geographic and geologic . . . "

The first significant influence of man on Grand Canyon ecosystems was that of the early prospectors. They came soon after Powell's entry into the region, roamed the farthest corners of the Canyon, built trails and camps and Heaven knows what else, and came away with little or no gold.

Their constant companions were burros, which are not even native to North America. Burros could live on the scant vegetation and limited water, and so served ideally as beasts of burden.

The wandering prospectors knew that bighorns and other desert creatures were already living a somewhat marginal existence in this environment, but they could see that the animals were well adapted to rigorous conditions. Whether these creatures could endure much outside competition, however, was not their major problem.

Had the miners taken their burros away with them, the natural scene might have retained its original status. But the burros were released, or lost, and in time the population of these animals rose to two thousand or more in this relatively small area.

The burros have been accused of fouling springs and destroying natural vegetation, but the full effects of their invasion are inadequately known. Some people think that burros and bighorns can live side by side successfully on the same natural range. If so, there is nothing wrong with that—provided that the range is outside a national park. Grand Canyon is for bighorns—and for associated species which time and evolution have developed to live in harmony with it.

The burros are still within the park, however, close to a hundred of them, and are extremely hard to get rid of. Like the goats of Hawaii and the mongooses of the Virgin Islands, they illustrate the troubles modern man has had, and continues to have, in undoing the careless or ignorant work of his ancestors.

Some early prospectors established their own private settlements at the edge of or within the Grand Canyon. Hundreds of claims were staked out. The miners built roads and trails, brought in dogs, mules, sheep, horses, even goldfish; they planted orchards and plowed lands for raising food, and constructed tents, cabins, camps, cableways, hotels, bunkhouses, corrals, warehouses, and bridges. Someone even built a distillery in the Canyon.

The miners shipped out tons of minerals, including asbestos and copper, and took stalactites and stalagmites out of caves.

Unfavorable economic factors brought an end to some of this, but the Canyon is still littered with debris of the mining era. Much of it is deemed historic today, and on that basis represents romantic aspects of exploration and exploitation. But if economic factors had been otherwise, if rocks and minerals could have been extracted profitably . . .

While miners were seeing what they could do within the Canyon, stockmen and hunters went to work on the rims. When man first came to the Kaibab Plateau, it was inhabited by an estimated three thousand Rocky Mountain mule deer. Hundreds of thousands of years of evolution had so dynamically and delicately balanced the plateau ecosystem that the deer population more or less matched vegetative conditions. When numbers of deer began to rise, enough wolves and mountain lions were around to cull the excess. Thus the vegetation, without severe browsing, developed very richly indeed.

This is an oversimplification of the matter, but the fact is that the forest was healthy. The deer were healthy. The predators were healthy.

Then came the white man. Seeing such an Elysium "going to waste," he imported two hundred thousand sheep, twenty thousand cattle and two thousand horses and pastured them on the luxuriant meadows and forest glades north of the north rim.

The stockgrowers knew, of course, that all these slow-moving domestic animals would be fair feast for predators, and so they enlisted all the help they could, including federally paid hunters, to track down and eliminate coyotes, lions, bobcats and wolves. This was done with efficiency and dispatch. In a few short years the predators practically vanished. One—the wolf—disappeared completely.

So did a great deal of grass. Gullies came into being on many parts of the plateau. Soils began washing away. It was all a familiar process, something man had been repeating for centuries: in Mesopotamia, the Anatolian Plateau, the French Alps, the South American chaco, and African savannas.

At first the livestock did not directly compete with the deer for food. Livestock ate grass. Deer usually browsed on trees and shrubs. But with the disappearance of grass, the livestock began to browse on trees and shrubs.

In a twisted tangle of events that came to a head during the winter of 1924–25, the natural fauna reacted in the only logical way it could. With predators gone, the deer multiplied beyond the capacity of the forest to supply food. They stretched as high as they could while standing on their hind legs, trying to get at the leaves that could give them life. Seedlings and shrubs within reach didn't have a chance.

There is no point going further into the details of this often-repeated story; the upshot of it was a massive enlistment of hunters to reduce the number of deer, and stricter measures to control the distribution of cattle.

This incident is famous for its lessons of wildlife management because it began to teach men how not to deal with wildlife populations; it demonstrated that wild animals must be carefully fitted

158

The Kaibab Trail crosses Hakatai Shale, inner gorge.

into the ecosystem of which they are a part and managed accordingly if a natural environment is to be sustained.

The lesson passed along to the rest of the world was simply that man had no more ability to create a Utopia for animals than for himself. It was embarrassing, of course, for Nature had again shown her superiority. The best environments were those man found upon arrival. Evolution, obviously, was going to be difficult to improve upon.

But man certainly tried. One of the most enduring images of the Kaibab affair is that of 125 men beating the bushes in an attempt to herd eight thousand mule deer down the trails and across the canyon to the south rim. It was an idea said to have originated with Zane Grey, the well-known western novelist, and the purpose was simply to reduce the Kaibab herd by relocation, a method more humane than shooting or starvation.

The deer were smarter than the men, however. They escaped the roundup, and not one cowboy got one deer even down into the Canyon, much less over to the other side.

Establishment of a national monument in 1908 and a national park in 1919 brought some measure of protection but no sudden solution to the problems. Neither did these actions bring man any nearer to know-how in the ways of wildlife.

They simply brought more men. Trails proliferated. Whereas in Powell's time few but Indian and animal paths existed, eventually men built some nineteen trails into the Canyon and otherwise facilitated human travel within it.

Roads were built on the rims and settlements, campgrounds, and other man-oriented facilities expanded or multiplied. To get enough water, men tapped springs within the Canyon and piped their waters hundreds of feet up the cliffs to the rims. They bridged the river and installed telephone lines into the Canyon.

Hotels, warehouses, homes, gardens, ranches, towers, tanks, museums, offices, curio shops, photo studios, corrals, garages, dumps, a railroad station, grocery stores, a post office, hospital, theater—man was not coming to this national park to get away from civilization. He was bringing it with him.

Upon administration by the National Park Service, protection became the first watchword. Wildfires that had raced across the forest for years, and had become a factor in the development of nearly every ecosystem on the rim, were almost completely suppressed. A highly efficient system of fire control went into operation.

Indeed, man apparently had no intention of simply observing what was here. He seemed bent on altering it.

These, of course, were the trying early years in which mistakes occurred, and men learned from some of them, as from the Kaibab deer incident. Modern hindsight has helped in other ways as well, and tourism is no longer as crucial as it was in order to attract widespread support. Many people, however, still mistakenly believe that the more names on the register, the more money Congress gives to administer the park.

As time went on, mule trips proliferated virtually *ad infinitum*. The major maintained trails grew more and more crowded with strings of mules carrying passengers and supplies. One group after another stretched out end to end up and down the trail. The lines of them grew longer until at last they were limited only by the number of mules that could be trained and the skills of the cowboys who could keep them shod.

Meanwhile, man modified the natural scene in other ways. The National Park Service undertook eradication of mistletoe from pine trees within a limited area of the park as a cooperative measure with the United States Forest Service. The purpose was to help protect forest and timber resources outside the park which were threatened by excessive growth and spread of mistletoe, which has a tendency to disfigure trees being produced for commercial purposes.

Forests within the park were beginning to suffer from a twist of fate that has become a hidden threat, and could become a serious, sudden danger. Because forest fires had been controlled for so many years, the build-up of underbrush became a critical problem because it had not been swept out or thinned away by natural fire. Were a conflagration to get well started, it could run away in a hotter fire than nature ever knew, and thus more thoroughly eliminate wildlife communities.

Controlled burning of the underbrush seems almost essential, but the risk is that if it should get out of control and wipe out a major section of ponderosa pine, it could also wipe out a sizable portion of wildlife populations as well. In the case of the Kaibab squirrel, that could be disastrous.

161

A hundred years ago, John Wesley Powell floated down an utterly wild river. The Colorado still has some of the wildest stretches of any river in the United States, but upstream from Grand Canyon it has been stopped by the Glen Canyon Dam. A reservoir, ironically named Lake Powell, has destroyed 186 miles of the river he loved so well, including such places as the famed Music Temple.

Downstream from the dam, within the Grand Canyon itself, the river has become utterly different and unpredictable—colder, clearer and for the most part a much less effective cutting tool in the erosion of the Canyon. Releases from the reservoir diminish on the weekends because of reduced demand for electricity. At such times the water flow goes down to around six thousand cubic feet per second, low enough to endanger boatmen running the river. They claim that in places they must have eleven to twelve thousand cubic feet per second or they can't run the rapids. Low water exposes too many rocks for safety.

If they beach their boat when the water is up and explore a side canyon, they may return to find the water down and their boat stranded. If heavy or full of provisions, it may be unmovable until the water rises again.

Or should the boat be beached at low water and a sudden surge of water is released at the dam while they are exploring, they could return to find the boat torn away and gone.

Water release charts are available, and to some extent fluctuating water levels can be predicted. But there are overriding and unpredictable factors, such as surges in power demand that take precedence over boat parties on the river. There is no guarantee. The river is no longer what it was.

Nor is the sky.

The sky that over Cheyava Falls we knew to be so clear and serene and beautiful—silent but alive with moving clouds—that sky, like the river, had turned into something else.

We had thought it to be as inviolate as the canyon. It had been one of the three essential elements that made up the total environment, the total experience, the deep and abiding spell: canyon, sky, and silence.

Now that, too, had changed. One morning in late September, well after the bulk of the summer tourist season was over and the Canyon, if only barely, had begun to settle down to the lesser routine of winter, we left the river to walk to the rim.

Twenty years had passed since the hike to Cheyava Falls. The memory and the wonder of that earlier trip, even the smallest details of it, had clung to us like the atmosphere to the earth, had revived

162

Sand and seep and mud below Tatahatso Point.

and renewed us on demand, had let us remember in times of stress that somewhere was a perfect place so quiet you could hear the song of a canyon wren a mile away.

Now on this September day we paused to watch the roiling river, to admire the empty sky, to soak up the silence and solitude. We recharged ourselves with whatever it is that man draws from such an environment to restore his soul and send him back to everyday life better equipped to cope.

By eight in the morning, accompanied by the songs of the canyon wren, we were well on the way, when suddenly an echoing, thundering, droning, vibrating roar came down the canyon. First from this direction, then from that, it pervaded the gorge. It surged from one wall to another, wavering and quivering, changing in volume. It seemed to come from all directions at once.

Suddenly a low-winged light plane appeared over the lip of the inner gorge, not two thousand feet overhead, the growl of its motor amplified within the echo chamber where we walked, and where there was little vegetation to absorb the sound.

The music of the canyon wren disappeared. The chatter of the rock squirrel died. The rumble of the river seemed to halt.

The plane passed out of sight, but for a long time afterward the echoes of its motor returned. Obviously it was circling. Side canyons above and below served as amplification channels to direct the sound to our ears. After a while it was gone.

A few minutes of silence. The primeval sound of the river returned. But no squirrel, no canyon wren.

Then, with a much more sudden roar, two military jets, in close formation, dived into the inner gorge, skimming the cliffs and breaking the silence with a piercing, shattering roar.

They were quickly gone. But still no squirrel or canyon wren: we wondered what effects such disturbances had on their reproductive cycles. We had no idea—what did any man know of animal stress?

164

The faint, familiar sound of high-flying commercial jets filled the canyon, reminders of a world we had come here to forget, a world beloved in many ways but still worth getting completely away from once in a while. If we could not get away from it in the bottom of the Grand Canyon, where else?

During the next four hours we made our way at a leisurely pace

Summer sky over the north rim.

out of the canyon, and it was simply one aircraft after another. More sightseeing planes. Another military jet. Regularly scheduled passenger flights taking off from Grand Canyon airport and zooming over the gorge. A helicopter. A light plane. Another helicopter . . .

Black clouds rolled up, and a storm broke at high noon, curtailing air traffic. But we had kept count. As we came out of the gorge—a time span of one-half day—thirty-five aircraft had flown over or into the Canyon, or both.

As it happened, we did not hear a sonic boom, but were told that they do occur and do cause damage. One broke a dining room plate glass window in the Grand Canyon Lodge on the north rim. The glass burst inward and caused considerable damage, fortunately at a time when no one was in the room. The glass has since been strengthened.

Although it is difficult to prove, park officials are certain that sonic booms have also caused rock slides, one of which took out part of a trail and made necessary substantial repairs. Booms used to be heard on the average of one a day, but seem to be diminishing, perhaps in response to public objections.

Sonic booms have plagued other parts of the country so severely that recording devices are being installed to measure the intensity and frequency of them. Worse yet, from Canyon de Chelly, not far to the east of the Grand Canyon, have come eye-witness reports of a sonic boom loosening a cliff that fell on a prehistoric Indian ruin and then plunged into a Navajo Indian cornfield.

Meanwhile, Grand Canyon Village grew and expanded, and by 1969 the annual visitation to the Canyon reached two million persons. Traffic impact on the Village became severe because the excessive modern traffic had to utilize roads and other facilities designed and built many years ago.

The Park's water problem became acute. Storage capacity was increased to fifteen million gallons, but since 65 per cent of the distribution system had become obsolete, breaks and leaks in pipes occurred repeatedly. Some water lines still in use date from 1904.

When demand at last exceeded supply, the springs at Indian Gardens, below the village, became inadequate. At that point the National Park Service decided to construct a pipeline all the way from Roaring Springs, under the north rim, to Grand Canyon Village on the south rim. The pipeline would cross the Colorado River on a new bridge less than a mile downstream from the existing suspension bridge on the Kaibab Trail. It would also be laid part way beneath existing trail bed.

By the time it was almost finished, in 1965, this project cost some $2.5 million.

Yet before it could be completed, the most severe flood in recorded history came down Bright Angel Canyon in 1966 and wiped out a good deal of the trail and the brand new pipeline.

The damage required nearly four years and over two million dollars more to repair.

A sewage treatment and water reclamation plant, installed in 1928, today treats several hundred thousand gallons of sewage every twenty-four hours, and the reclaimed water is used in irrigation, construction, comfort stations, wherever there is no chance of transferring harmful viruses to human beings—a remote possibility anyway because of the thorough treatment provided.

Extra heavy travel to the park has increased maintenance burdens in other ways. The National Park Service has to spend upwards of $25,000 a year to pick up litter along the roads. In addition to this, litter is retrieved in the course of other work and around residential and commercial areas. The total may run over $50,000 and the problem is worsening.

This is not solely because travel is increasing, however; it sometimes seems that people are simply getting more careless. Visitors throw a great deal of refuse over the rim, perhaps confident that it is disposed of forever; but park maintenance men periodically go over the edge on ropes in order to retrieve it and keep the Canyon clean. If only industry would make more containers that dissolved!

Disposal of all this refuse is a headache. It has to be ditch-trenched and buried—but ditches cannot be dug in the solid Kaibab limestone; they have to be blasted. Burning is out of the question, for polluting Canyon air is polluting the spell, the scenery, and the whole milieu.

The National Park Service has tried in desperation to make some arrangement for disposing of this great load of debris. But who else wants it?

One of the worst of all problems is the campground, thanks to more intense use, litter, vandalism, and noise. If drivers of trailer campers cannot find a regular space they may drive right out into the woods. Not needing established tables and fireplaces, they try to park wherever they please, seeking shade and grass. Such intrusions

167

push the wilderness buffer zone farther and farther back from the road or campground.

The National Park Service installs huge rocks, some as large as a car, to restrict passage beyond certain points. Yet people will move these rocks, determined to go beyond the barriers.

Such actions result in almost permanent damage to the natural ecosystem, because in this high-elevation, semiarid climate, vegetative recovery is very slow.

"We closed one of our campground loops for two years," a maintenance specialist told us in 1969. "We seeded it, fertilized it, scraped it, harrowed it, did everything but irrigate. Some grass came up. Then we turned the campers back in, and within two weeks it looked just like it had two years before."

Employee housing has become so tight that there has never been sufficient space for a full staff, and for that reason old structures become too valuable to tear down. Some houses sink to so low a standard that it becomes extremely difficult to ask anyone to live in them. Yet in some cases the need for more staff to handle more visitors compels the National Park Service to add new bedrooms to buildings that should have been torn down years ago.

And visitors keep arriving, by every conceivable means. So many floated down the Colorado River in the summer of 1968—nearly three thousand persons—that the National Park Service had to install a ranger river patrol. A crew was assigned to a rubber vessel and, despite the fluctuating, unpredictable releases of water from Glen Canyon Dam, made five patrols between May and September of that year.

Some thirty commercial river-running companies have been organized, each taking parties through the Canyon under permit by the National Park Service. Some use pontoon boats thirty-five feet long and take more than 120 persons through at a time.

Boating parties have long been required to clean up after themselves but the traffic has simply become too great to maintain a clean and natural river environment. The few available beaches are too small to accept one large crowd after another.

It is thus that a step toward civilizing the river has become essential. At two locations, Nankoweap and Tuckup Canyons, where traffic usually concentrates and many persons step ashore, primitive outdoor rest rooms have been installed.

Tamarix colonizes the dunes near Nankoweap Creek, Marble Gorge.

Park officials are fully cognizant that a little more of this sort of thing can affect the wilderness spell along the river. They are therefore attempting to determine just how many persons can go down the river without disturbing the pristine qualities that still remain. The question is: By what means do you measure such things?

The task may become inordinately difficult, yet park officials have no choice but to persevere. They know the problem as well as anyone, and will tell you if you ask: "We have a limited resource down there."

The whole park is a limited resource. At the same time there seems to be no end to the expansion of visitation figures. By 1978, the National Park Service expects more than three million visits annually to Grand Canyon National Park. By the end of the century the number could double.

Meanwhile the private promotional brochures proclaim: "Mule trail conquest." "Helicopter Cinerama." "Airplane spectacular."

Can the Canyon take it? Ecologists are apt to recall the axiom that a flower, fondled by too many fingers, wilts. The beauty of this great ecosystem, like that of a flower, is a fragile beauty that can only exist where fragile things are loved and cherished and kept undisturbed.

Some park officials would like nothing more than to cherish and keep unimpaired this domain for which they have responsibility. But they have little control over man's insatiable desire for "progress," which continues to plague the wilderness of the Grand Canyon.

On various occasions since the turn of the century there have been public skirmishes over proposals to inundate parts of the Canyon with waters backed up by dams constructed outside the park. These proposals were easy to understand and quick to attract the public scrutiny. They were defeated, and here and there one heard or read a pronouncement of victory. But the public now appears to possess a rather uneasy feeling that the battle over reservoirs is but a single encounter in a larger and more subtle war, that national parks may be endangered by serious threats that are as yet not widely understood, or perhaps even recognized.

That problem is not new, of course; nor is it limited to the Grand Canyon. Yosemite National Park in California has long had a reservoir. Glacier Bay National Monument in Alaska is completely open to mining exploration. Many parks have unsightly private inholdings that must be purchased and added to the park.

The situation is worse in certain other countries. National parks in some have been invaded by illegal settlers. War has devastated Garamba National Park in the Congo. A full-scale hydroelectric project has mushroomed in Kosciusko National Park, Australia. And in national parks in Venezuela, Turkey, and Canada, the skyline and the forest have been disfigured by the construction of tramways.

Some of the enthusiasm to build resorts within the national parks of the United States has been restrained. But the Grand Canyon has been confronted by persons with a burning desire to get to the bottom and back in as short a time as possible, and the park has had its share of visitors and public officials who advocated quick descent.

The idea of building tramways, elevators, and inclined railways has been around for decades. Certain members of Congress have disposed of such matters as being dangerous precedent-setters that would "do great violence" to the traditional policy of preserving the pristine character of parks, and have denied their installation, which seems to be in accord with the wishes of the public at large.

Nevertheless, some influential people, including other members of Congress, continue to pursue the idea. They believe that if the parks are not used to the "fullest possible extent" they are not being used as the original mandates implied, and therefore additional methods of access ought to be provided. They feel that tramways are one answer, and are convinced that cables and support structures can be "hidden so well they could not be seen from the rims," and therefore "would not interfere with the scenery." Whether or not one tramway would suffice is seldom mentioned. However, a top Canyon official once told us: "I want eight of them!"

This seems always to have been a minority view, though it is vigorously espoused from time to time. The dangers of setting a precedent are easy to recognize; few other installations would so fully destroy the spell of Canyon wildness.

In this connection it is amusing and instructive to recall the Congressional testimony of men who in 1910 sought legislation to build a tunnel down through the rocks to accommodate an inclined railroad into the Canyon: **171**

Mr. Herrick. In the tunnel we would need about 8 feet; maybe a little more.
Mr. Oppmann. At first it would be just as wide as a street-car track. But our expectation is that just as soon as it becomes known and the tunnel is excavated so that people can go down into it there will be

more traffic than ever before. Then it would be necessary to have two tracks, one going and one coming. Do you understand?

The Chairman. A double-track right of way would be about 50 feet?

Mr. Oppmann. About 50 feet. I think that would be a fair width.

There are other places where such things can be installed, and indeed have been. Devotees of tramways, frontier villages, roadside zoos, and outdoor theaters may find them concentrated conveniently in small areas, such as Palo Duro Canyon State Park, Texas, or adjacent to scenic areas in other localities.

All signs seem to point to a well-rooted conservation consciousness (some call it an ethic) within the United States. There has in fact been an almost complete reversal of the opinion expressed in the 1910 Congressional hearings by one of the proponents of the Grand Canyon railway:

All this talk about destroying the beauties of this mighty gorge is all stuff and nonsense to anyone who has gazed into its awful and mysterious depths. It is so limitless and mighty that man's puny hand can not mar it, any more than it can dim a star in the heavens. By comparison a silk thread stretched from the Dome of the Capitol to Mount Vernon would ruin the beauties of the Potomac and commercialize the atmosphere about the grave of Washington.

Such ironies are obvious. The cruder proposals are containable. Less apparent and more significant, however, are the long-term effects of too many visits, too many river parties, too many mules and burros, too many aircraft, too many dams, too much urban influence, too much zeal. These are the problems of today and tomorrow, and we shall proceed now to discuss how each is being solved.

And it is high time to solve them. Had John Wesley Powell been around on the centennial of his river exploration he might well have wondered:

"What will another hundred years of man do to the Grand Canyon?"

12

TRIAL AND ERROR

Looking on in despair, Theodore Roosevelt, if he could be here, might think that no one had ever listened to him. Do nothing to mar it, he said, but as we have seen, the Grand Canyon has indeed been marred.

The situation might look hopeless, as though the tide is too great to turn. But not so.

The first tendency is to criticize the National Park Service for inequities, faults, and slippages in management of the park, and for doing nothing about the problems. This criticism is easy because the Service is visible and vulnerable—a place to lay the blame for overall failings of science and society.

Of course, the Service also has immediate responsibility—but it by no means has final responsibility. Nor does the United States Congress. Those who accuse either or both eventually find themselves accusing the image in the mirror. For the final authority lies with the people themselves, a fact not as abstract as it sounds.

The National Park Service at the park-management level is composed not of brutal bureaucrats, as they are sometimes called, but of some of the most practical, hard-working, dedicated men and women in public service. They work an enormous number of hours of uncompensated overtime, and by doing so in effect contribute hundreds of thousands of dollars to the United States Treasury. This can be verified not only by scanning official records and management surveys but by just watching rangers, naturalists, maintenancemen, and managers at work. They perform their duties not on orders from above or out of loyalty to superiors, but out of a love of job and park, perhaps a loyalty to and respect for animals and solitude and natural beauty more than anything else.

It is almost a measurable devotion. The late Senator Harry Byrd liked to say that the Service gave back $1.20 value for every dollar appropriated to it.

Many park employees at the Canyon know no limits to their official duty hours. Some are on call twenty-four hours a day. They are 60 miles from the nearest town of any substantial size (aside from Grand Canyon Village) and 230 miles from Phoenix. They stick to their jobs on highly irregular schedules, subject to public command. They cancel their personal plans when a rescue has to be made or an official visit is scheduled. They have innumerable VIP's to usher around, some of whom require hours or days of personal service, ranger assistance, or rides from here to there.

They endure such things with a smile because their park and their work supersede all else, and they have a special camaraderie, sometimes an exceptionally high morale. If they err, it is likely to be on the side of wanting to do too much for visitors or to protect visitors too much. To control this zeal, there is a continuing need for persuasive guidance, and such guidance comes most usefully, accurately and honestly from the public.

Of course, Congress is sometimes the instrument for transmission of this guidance, but letters from the public often go directly to the service. However transmitted, suggestions sooner or later arrive at the park and are taken into consideration during staff planning sessions. Attacks are unnecessary. As Lucretius said, "The short song of the swan is better than the loud noise of cranes."

If the average citizen thinks there is no room for his views in park management, let him be reassured that the National Park Service, ever sensitive to public reaction, keeps its policy interpretations flexible, though they are based on the law of the land and can stretch only so far.

174   On one side of the Service are people, including members of Congress who control park budgets, advocating new modes of access in addition to roads and trails. They profess an inability to understand why ardent conservationists (among whom are included other members of Congress) consistently reject such proposals.

They want to improve and expand park use, but at the same time avoid impairment of park values. They are aware that a saturation point can be reached, but feel that innovations should be examined and that somehow there should be access to what they call vast untapped areas of existing national parks.

On the other side of the Service are persons who consider that the untapped areas are accessible enough—and ought to be left untapped. Such in fact is the principle behind the Wilderness Act of 1964, which states:

A wilderness, in contrast with those areas where man and his own works dominate the landscape, is hereby recognized as an area where the earth and its community of life are untrammeled by man, where man himself is a visitor who does not remain. An area of wilderness is further defined to mean in this Act an area of undeveloped Federal land retaining its primeval character and influence, without permanent improvements or human habitation, which is protected and managed so as to preserve its natural conditions and which (1) generally appears to have been affected primarily by the forces of nature, with the imprint of man's work substantially unnoticeable; (2) has outstanding opportunities for solitude or a primitive and unconfined type of recreation; (3) has at least five thousand acres of land or is of sufficient size as to make practicable its preservation and use in an unimpaired condition; and (4) may also contain ecological, geological, or other features of scientific, educational, scenic, or historical value.

There are many articulate spokesmen for the view that Congress did not intend national parks to be opened up to vast hordes of people, lest they destroy the very things parks were meant to preserve.

"All museums are not ensconced in marble halls," said straight-talking conservationist Ernie Swift; "nor does anyone roller skate in an art gallery. Our public leadership is allowing the intrinsic values of the national parks and monuments to deteriorate because a few false prophets are preaching a new gospel. . . . We cannot allow the toys which have been invented to enhance recreation to take precedence over everything which nature has to offer. There are places in this land where primitive nature must not be treated as an obstruction."

Other citizens are more fervent. One wrote to us: "We have heard enough of this 'parks are for people' pitch. What they mean by that is that parks are for motors, with people on them."

The National Park Service has, of course, established a number of policies regarding these problems, but the public is not always sure that Service policies are, or can be, fully enforced. Stewart M. Brandborg, executive director of the Wilderness Society, maintains

175

that the public is "far out in front of the average government land manager who resigns himself to the invasion by a flood of humanity that could destroy the natural areas."

James B. Craig, of the American Forestry Association, says that the pressure of people on land is great and, in his words, bureaucrats, politicians, and business types are often fragile reeds who bend to pressures not necessarily in the public interest.

Let us now examine a few of the general guidelines that enable the National Park Service to deal with problems that have developed at the Grand Canyon.

From experience, the Service has developed policies for the natural areas under its administration, which account for 94 per cent of the thirty million acres of the national park system.

"The *preservation* of natural areas," says published Service policy, "is a fundamental requirement for their use and enjoyment as *unimpaired* natural areas. Park management, therefore, looks first to the care and management of the natural resources of a park. The concept of preservation of a total environment, as compared with the protection of an individual feature or species, is a distinguishing feature of national park management."

Ideally, the Service would like to do this by using an ecological approach that would neutralize the unnatural influences of man and thereby enable natural environments to maintain themselves. For example, missing native species of flora and fauna would be reintroduced wherever possible; while nonnative species—and this would include the burros of the Grand Canyon—would be controlled "where feasible" when they threaten invasion of a natural area. The Service hedges in this regard; total elimination of exotics would be very costly.

Forest fires, when not dangerous to man or facilities, are natural and could be allowed to burn, thus improving the natural scene. Prescribed burning is being increasingly employed in other places to restore a natural ecosystem to what it was before man stopped all fires. Commercial harvesting of timber, of course, is not allowed.

176

Motorized vehicles are permitted on roads but not on trails. Extraction of minerals is not allowed unless authorized by laws left over from the early mining era.

Service policy is still to be developed fully in the area of noise abatement, aircraft overflights, and the use of motorized water craft.

A pioneering globemallow stabilizes the sand near Nankoweap Creek.

Air pollution from campfires, refuse burning and other kinds of combustion (auto exhausts are not specified) "will be controlled in public-use areas to the extent necessary to maintain clean air."

Hunting and the collection of plants and rocks are prohibited. Sport fishing, which the United Nations does not countenance in its criteria for national park uses, has been traditionally approved in United States national parks. While accepted by a majority, and engaged in by only a very small percentage of park visitors, the act of fishing seems to be inconsistent with the national park idea.

The wildlife management program is based on control of animal populations by natural predation. If additional control must be initiated, as for example when animal populations grow too large for the ecosystem to support, such measures as live trapping and direct reduction by National Park Service personnel are taken.

Sound management of any national park usually means that exploitation and private uses must be eliminated by acquisition of private lands within its boundaries. The policy states that if existing incompatible uses persist, or new ones arise:

... the Service will attempt to negotiate with the owner for the acquisition of the property in order to eliminate a use or avoid development of a use adverse to the management of the area. In the event all reasonable efforts at negotiation fail and the owner persists in his efforts to devote the property to a use deemed by the Service to be adverse to the primary purpose for which the area was established, the United States will institute eminent domain proceedings to acquire the property and eliminate such use or prevent such development.

Back-pack camping by individuals, families, and groups is encouraged, but the policy says that where the intensity of such use threatens values for which each park was established, the Service will provide camp sites, trailside shelters, and minimum sanitary facilities. Some persons feel strongly, of course, that the facilities themselves threaten park values. On this score, there is a policy that says groups of people may be limited in size and the frequency of visits kept down if necessary.

Thus, despite its statements of general policy, the Service keeps most options open. The danger is that policies acceptable in one park may be unacceptable in another. The park staffs maintain their own vigilance, but continuing public review is vital.

To help keep down the need for sanitary paraphernalia, campers may be required to pack out noncombustible trash. However, maintenance experts who follow the trends foresee little hope in voluntary public cleanup.

As for aircraft and float trips, the over-all policy states that where aircraft operations adversely affect the environment of a natural area, the cooperation of agencies exerting flight control over aircraft will be sought to institute such measures as will minimize or eliminate the disturbance. The use of aircraft in natural areas is permissible in the saving of human life or the protection of threatened park resources, or when the use of aircraft offers significant advantages to area management and such can be accomplished with minimum disturbance to visitor enjoyment. Some persons, however, question the National Park Service's competence to judge such matters, especially what constitutes "minimum disturbance."

"Float-equipped or amphibious aircraft may land in designated water-oriented parks to provide visitor access to selected areas. Landings will be restricted to waters especially designated on the park Master Plan for this use." Master plans, however, are technical documents that have not always been prepared with assistance from the private sector, though they are open for public inspection.

The fundamental policy is that outdoor recreation in natural areas —hiking, climbing, sightseeing, winter- and water-use activities, nature observation, picnicking, photography and so on—are encouraged and facilitated where they do not materially alter or disturb the environment or introduce undue artificiality.

Parks are also for advancement of scientific knowledge, according to government policy, and constitute comparatively pure natural ecosystems of great value in basic research—providing, again, that the natural integrity is not itself impaired.

The National Park Service is wary of long-range road and traffic policies, since public views are changing rapidly in this field. The Service feels that the purpose of traffic management should be to enhance the quality of a park experience, a relatively unarguable premise—as long as there must be traffic. Only in one national park, Isle Royale in Michigan, are motor vehicles excluded.

179

Still, the gap between good policies and good execution of them varies in direct ratio to public response, Congressional pressure and/or appropriations, and creative Federal management. Some persons say that appropriations are too small, some say they are too large. Park officials from other countries, observing what they consider to be too many developments in the national parks, have said: "You are getting too much money."

Creative Federal management is spotty and its quality varied, just as in private enterprise; nor do Federal employees have complete freedom to innovate.

Thus it seems clear that national park policy evolves as public thinking evolves on these matters, though critics say that national park policy lags decades behind.

The National Park Service, being conservative, cannot use such fighting words as Richard Means, an instructor of sociology at Kalamazoo College, Michigan, did in an article for the *Saturday Review*. In his essay, Means touched on attempts

. . . to dam and flood mile after mile of the Grand Canyon in order to produce more electricity—a commodity we seem to have in great abundance. The Grand Canyon, of course, is not a commodity; it is truly, in popular parlance, a "happening." Uncontrolled by man, created by nature, it cannot be duplicated. Any assault on its natural state is an equal attack on man's capacity to wonder, to contemplate his environment and nature's work. In short, such activities seem to belittle and diminish man himself. Thus the activities of those who suggest such destruction assume a restricted view of man and his capacity for joy in nature. In this sense, such activities are immoral. We could lengthen the list, but it should be clear that destruction of nature by man's gratuitous "busyness" and technological arrogance is the result of a thoughtless and mindless human activity.

The noted author Robert Cahn once conducted a park survey in connection with a series of articles he wrote for the *Christian Science Monitor*, which won for him the Pulitzer Prize in general reporting. At the close of the series, entitled "Will Success Spoil the National Parks?" Cahn conducted a survey and obtained some clear messages from the public: Take campgrounds out of the parks or at least set up some limits to and in them; limit expansion of park concessions and "entertainment"; slow down on road-building in national parks; leave the wilderness alone; and do something to offset man's influence on the natural scene.

One respondent said: "We cannot now afford travel to national parks, but it's nice to think that they will be there if ever we can."

A 1969 Gallup Poll conducted for the National Wildlife Federa-

Water-worn wall in Monument Canyon.

tion covered a carefully selected sample of 1,500 men and women across the country. According to the poll, they were deeply concerned about destruction of the environment and would be willing to pay more taxes to clean up their surroundings. Most thought that either air or water pollution (or both) constituted the most pressing environmental problems and that the best ways to correct them were to control auto exhaust, chemical and industrial wastes, and smoke. The poll also suggested that most persons would support wildlife preservation through one or more of three major methods: enforcement of game laws, reduction in hunting, and establishment of parks and wildlife refuges—which tends to bolster the opinion of persons who consider that parks are for animals.

It thus seems clear what the trend is, and that Henry Van Dyke anticipated it when he said, "A National park should be as sacred as a temple."

Indeed, the public seems to be saying that national parks should be treated like cathedrals—heavily used but deeply respected; well attended but never violated or desecrated.

If we consider that the Grand Canyon is also a living museum of ecology, a natural library of geology, and an art gallery of kaleidoscopic scenes and sculptures, then we would treat it as we treat museums, libraries, or art galleries.

National parks are special. They are not playgrounds for human beings, or bedrooms, or ranches, resorts, circuses, communes, convention centers, hunting and collecting preserves, fairgrounds, sporting rinks, or centers for experimental technology. There are thousands of places outside the national parks where such things exist, or could exist, without disturbing the finest examples of the nation's natural heritage.

Thus we see what national parks are intended to be, what people of today think they ought to be, and what some of the policies are that govern them. Let us see now whether or not those policies, in combination with new ideas, can solve some of the problems at the Grand Canyon.

13

RESCUE

"THE GRAND CANYON is a land of song," wrote John Wesley Powell. Today the Canyon is still a land of song—when the planes are not flying—and efforts are under way to undo the damage of the past.

Mining properties within the park are reverting, one by one, to the government. The railroad is closing down operations; passenger runs have been abandoned and freight service is only intermittent.

The rim on which several buildings are located is railroad land, and United States attorneys believe that when it is no longer being used for railroad purposes it will revert from its land grant status to the property of the United States.

Park personnel are attempting to replace or eliminate antiquated water lines. They hope someday to convert the park sign system into safer breakaway types and utilize symbols that conform to international standards—or, better yet, eliminate private vehicles altogether. Attempts are being made to place all wire lines underground, using products that will resist everything except earthquakes and cost 95 per cent less to maintain than overhead wires.

They would also like to encourage wilderness devotees to shun those trails that have too many mules and too many people, but before doing so would like to make the other trails in the park a little safer.

Litter, deterioration, the needs of a city within a park—all require a full-time staff of sixty maintenance men and an extra forty in the summer. Even that is not enough; the "backlog of deferred maintenance" is no joke to those who are trying to keep park facilities safe for visitors. Yet the problems continue, abetted by rising costs, and park officials see little relief in sight.

The fundamental challenge at present is how to provide for large numbers of people, and give to each person a meaningful experience, yet restore as much as possible of the original spell of the Canyon.

One often hears the proposal that reduction in numbers of visitors to levels of a decade or so ago would help bring back the wilderness that existed then. Some persons are tempted to take the easy route and simply "reduce the hordes" that visit the Canyon, setting up some kind of reservation system to deter and restrain. That step may be necessary someday, perhaps sooner rather than later, and certainly some thought will have to be given to it by the next generation of managers. The 1916 Act of Congress establishing the National Park Service makes clear that use will be both promoted and regulated.

In the meantime, we ought to be able to solve the problem without severe reduction in human opportunity to get at least a glimpse of the Canyon. The example of Great Smoky Mountains National Park, most heavily visited national park in the United States, indicates that there is no reason why Grand Canyon could not retain its values with thrice the number of visits it now gets annually—but there would have to be some modifications to present practices, and perhaps some sharp restrictions on public use.

The fact is that the Grand Canyon is eighth among all national parks in number of visits per year, and persons who say that it and other parks like Yellowstone and Yosemite are crowded usually mean that the roads and parking lots are crowded. Troubles arise when too many cars go inside a park and too many people enter the fragile wilderness areas that are not supposed to be teeming with people. Visitors are indeed going farther into the wilderness, even in the Grand Canyon. Campgrounds in the bottom of the Canyon are jammed on holiday weekends, and the use of nonmaintained trails is increasing steadily.

184 A critical question is: How many of the millions of people who come to the Grand Canyon really wanted to be there in the first place? Perhaps they should have realized before arriving, or at least been told, that the Grand Canyon is not for everyone.

Comments against it are legion. Early trappers said that the river was caged and pent up in "horrid mountains." Lieutenant Ives left the enduringly classic opinion that after entering this region there was nothing to do but leave.

Relatively speaking, few people have any desire to enter the Canyon. Van Dyke said that from the comfort of the rim you look out, perhaps indolently coming to the conclusion that you are seeing the whole Canyon, and nine out of ten people rest content with that view and that conclusion. At any one point, he said, there are enough marvels for an afternoon.

Some people have no interest whatever in even coming to the Canyon (though they would fight with vigor to prevent its despoliation). "Kindly tell me why I should ever want to go there," one friend said to us. "Dozens of people have told me what it looks like. I have seen innumerable pictures of it. I therefore know exactly what it is like in summer, winter, spring and fall, inside and out. Now give me one solid reason why I should actually visit the place. My own experience could not exceed, by far, all that I have read about it, and I don't have to stand on the rim amid the jostle of crowds."

We recently asked a member of the British Parliament what he thought of the Canyon. "Well," he replied candidly, looking down into the gorge, "I can't actually say it's as smashing as all that. Your Arches National Monument is much more terrific."

We have heard hundreds of complaints about the Canyon.

"Much overrated."

"I don't understand it. Incomprehensible."

"I'll take Oak Creek Canyon any time."

"Zion Canyon is for me. You feel closer to it."

We have also repeatedly seen people who dared not get within twenty feet of the rim, people petrified with an acrophobic fear that they might, uncontrollably, jump in. They actually feared the Canyon, as if it stirred in them some wholly inhuman dementia.

People have come up to us and said, in a shaken voice, "I was just standing there, and suddenly I felt myself falling forward, right over the edge! If I hadn't caught myself in time, I don't know what would have happened. It just seemed like the Canyon was pulling me in. I can't believe it."

Such reactions are fairly common. Many a visitor has had to pull himself away from the rim, weak and trembling, and find a place to sit so that he could put himself together again.

Dutton cited reactions of shock, oppression, and horror, and said that persons could be doomed to disappointment, or be resentful, bewildered, and confused. The Canyon at night, according to poets, has "moaning winds" that give it a "ghostly aspect."

From all this we might conclude that persons in doubt about whether they should visit the Canyon shouldn't.

Rangers at entrance stations sometimes are asked: "Is it really worth driving on in to see?" That question is difficult for a ranger to answer objectively—he probably regards it as worth driving thousands of miles to see. There should be some more neutral and disinterested means of presenting advice, some means of telling potential visitors what the Canyon is *not*: not a resort, not an amusement park, not a recreation area, not a hunting ground, and so on. These are all negative—but as it is now they are rarely combined with the positive points to give the traveler a balanced view. A travel agent could hardly be expected to do it. Neither could the State of Arizona. We are still under the influence of Theodore Roosevelt's dictum that everybody should see this place.

Time has shown that that isn't so. Or else time is producing new conditions that Roosevelt didn't anticipate.

Public Enemy Number One is the automobile. There are persons who feel that private autos have no business in any national park. They suggest the substitution of shuttle buses (preferably operating on some kind of steam or electric system, or on an internal-combustion engine that does not pollute the air). These buses could bring visitors into the park every ten minutes or so and drop them off at various stations along the route.

The operators of Colonial Williamsburg, in Virginia, have so well perfected this system that it could be adapted to fit the needs of the Canyon. Private cars, all kept outside the boundary of the national park, could hardly spoil the canyon environment. Car passengers could decide where along the route they wished to leave the buses, could spend an hour or a day as they preferred, and then be picked up at the same or a different stop. Food services could be limited to what is becoming a popular trend anyway—quick-access snacks—and there would be no overnight facilities. With cars parked at the boundary, major services could be located there, too.

186

This possibility has long been discussed. Some people see it as inevitable, and there are times when rangers would certainly like to see the troublesome city environment removed from the park. Indeed, it would be ironic if we went on and on until we had another massive housing development inside the park, designed as nothing more, in the words of René Dubos, than disposable cubicles for dispensable people.

A well-financed developer could open a satellite village outside the park. Gatlinburg, Tennessee, affords an example; its proximity makes facilities within Great Smoky Mountains National Park unnecessary, and keeps the park almost entirely for pure enjoyment of the things for which it was set aside.

Another way of dispersing some of the pressure might be for the Indians themselves—Hualapais and Navajos—to develop tourist facilities near where their own lands abut the Canyon. The Navajo Tribe already has a growing tribal parks system.

Congress has always taken an interest in the operation of hotels and other facilities within the parks. An act of 1965 (PL 89-249) referred to early legislation in order to point out that the fundamental purpose of the national parks was to conserve their scenery, wildlife, natural and historic objects, and provide for their enjoyment in ways that will leave them unimpaired for future generations. Then it went on to say:

The Congress hereby finds that the preservation of park values requires that such public accommodations, facilities, and services as have to be provided within those areas should be provided only under carefully controlled safeguards against unregulated and indiscriminate use, so that the heavy visitation will not unduly impair those values and so that development of such facilities can best be limited to locations where the least damage to park values will be caused. It is the policy that such development shall be limited to those that are necessary and appropriate for public use and enjoyment of the national park area in which they are located and that are consistent to the highest practicable degree with the preservation and conservation of the areas.

The key phrase seems to be "necessary and appropriate," which is again where the citizen comes in. What is necessary? What is appropriate?

Taken to an extreme, the concession concept could be extended to campgrounds so that they would be developed with a luxuriousness on par with that permitted in hotels and likewise be managed by concessioners. But that has been experimented with, and the line seems to be drawn against such an extension. In fact, many people are drawing a solid line even further—against extension of *any* manmade facilities in national parks.

Accordingly, it would be logical to assume that if public demand for services and facilities can be better met outside the park—where more luxury and more variety can be supplied—and the public wants it that way, then such things within parks should be abandoned and

187

the sites allowed to revert to their natural state, campgrounds included.

The issue of camp sites in national parks has been heatedly raised by nongovernmental individuals and organizations. There are now more privately owned and operated campgrounds in the United States than public—Federal, state, and local combined. Private-campground owners feel that they hold the key to a better future for the camping public because they can install a large number of hookups, swimming pools, recreation halls, and the like to supply a luxury-minded generation that comes to "camp" in recreational vehicles. Campground developers outside national parks who need more land for expansion are willing to buy it and provide what the public wants.

Indeed, private enterprise has cashed in on the recreation boom, as witness the growth of campground chains that have proliferated like shopping centers. But private operators complain about what they see as unfair competition, saying that public campgrounds are advertised on a privileged basis, subject to less strict regulations, rented to campers for lower fees, and developed with tax-supported capital investment.

The private sector recommends that, if a public campground must exist, its facilities should be primitive. They point out that camping is a means, not an end—which suggests that national parks should be devoted primarily to management and protection of the "end." Indeed, some outsiders would like to "free the Park Service's field staff from playing nursemaid to campers and make them available for duties associated with truly fulfilling the purposes of the parks."

The rangers and naturalists we have talked with could not agree more. They look longingly at official policy which states that, where adequate concession facilities and services exist or can be developed by private enterprise outside national parks, such things shall not be provided within the natural areas.

188 Commercial camping people think this ought to apply to camp-grounds as well. Speaking before the annual convention of the National Campground Owners Association in Cleveland, Ohio, in 1968, Curtis G. Fuller, president of Woodall Publishing Company, said:

We must consider the difficult problem of what happens when space does not permit the development or extension of campgrounds within the parks. Or that even when space is available the park roads themselves are so jammed they can't handle the choke of recreational vehicle traffic. Here it is proposed . . . that family camping activity might better be left to private enterprise outside the park—probably at or near the entrances to the parks. This would be especially true when the park itself offered some popular attraction that drew campers in such numbers that their very presence might help destroy the attraction for which they came. We have to face the fact that this is actually happening in many of our parks.

If the urban environment of the village could be moved outside the boundary of Grand Canyon National Park, then the National Park Service might be able to abandon its old and obsolete water mains, remove some of the storage tanks, tear up pipelines within the Canyon itself, and relieve the rangers of urban police responsibilities.

Transportation snarls would almost if not totally disappear. Park personnel might not be plagued by old and obsolete housing or substandard traffic patterns. Trucks would not deliver supplies to grocery stores or mail to the post office or machines to garages. The government would not have to underwrite the expense of installing smokeless incinerators or blasting refuse pits in solid limestone.

These accouterments of civilization would be outside the park, five miles or more from the rim, far enough through the forest to eliminate some of the noise and noxious fumes. With that the forest ecosystem would in every likelihood improve, and there would be a substantial return of the primeval silence with which the Canyon was endowed for millions of years before man.

Providing, of course, that something is also done about aircraft. Surely it is a beautiful and exhilarating experience to see the Grand Canyon by air, and one might be tempted to allow overflights during, say, one hour of the day—a sort of fly-over hour which everybody could expect.

But mature reflection should show that flights over the Canyon are simply unnecessary. Standing on the rim a person is already 5,000 feet above the floor of the Canyon. Aerial looks into hidden corners of canyons could be satisfied by other means. If the urge to swoop down into scenic canyons is irresistible, then perhaps some other place in the American Southwest could be set aside for that purpose.

189

The only permissible course of action at the Grand Canyon, it seems to us, should be the complete elimination of overflights, including a slight rerouting of commercial transcontinental flights. Jets are familiar everywhere, but silence is not.

And the river? Should boats as well as autos and planes be removed from the national park? The question is whether, by noise or numbers, they violate the solitude of the Canyon. Motorboats do disturb, of course, and should by all means be eliminated from the Colorado River within the park.

Even without motors, there are limits. Thousands of boats going down the river every day, and consequent disturbance by landing parties, might have a grave effect on natural ecosystems along the way.

Boat trips, pack trips, mule trips, all will have to be kept within bounds. Autos, airplanes, and motorboats will almost certainly have to be removed.

And then there are avant-garde vehicles such as snowmobiles, hovercraft, trail breakers, and all-terrain machines. Ample area outside national parks should be available for these types of transport. And in the not-too-distant future we shall face the problems inherent in "all-air" craft, the flying-belt generation. This matter will be handled by our sons and their sons, and the best we can do now is set a wise and foreseeing precedent.

As Theodore Roosevelt said of the Grand Canyon: Leave it as it is.

"Lock it up" is how the liberal-minded might interpret that statement and they could well be justified in pointing out that restricting visitors to national parks borders on the illegal. Again the familiar question returns: How can millions more people be admitted and given an understanding and appreciation of this park?

One solution often heard is that a computerized reservation system such as that used by air lines and hotel chains be placed in effect to hold back human crowds that threaten fragile natural areas. Some persons say that limits, even if arbitrary, should be established and visitors allowed on a first-come, first-served basis, but when the limits are reached the gates will be closed. Cartoonists have already touched upon this point. Such restrictions would be legal on the basis that the park's resources were being threatened.

There are practical ways, however, to sustain high-density human use without impairing the park. Some have been tested. Certain fragile parts of the park could be closed periodically, as happens to bird rookeries in tropical parks at nesting time. Or parts could be closed permanently; Montezuma Castle, an ancient Indian ruin south of the Grand Canyon, was closed years ago lest trampling shake it off the side of the cliff in which it had built. Ways and means have also been tried to encourage wider use during seasons other than summer, as for example winter hikes or spring flowering pilgrimages.

Perhaps another section of the park could be devеlóped for public use, as has been done at Mesa Verde National Park. There is dangerous precedent for this sort of thing at the Grand Canyon, however, recalling some of the adverse comments about the canyon: if you see what can be seen from the dozens of vista points already accessible by road, you are likely to have had enough of the Grand Canyon. Why open more?

Indeed, why disperse the crowds at all? If people can be concentrated along the overlooks now available, if one highway can link the rim with the boundary, and if quiet buses can move people in and out on a rapid shuttle system, then a great many people can come in for an hour's look or a day's touring. And chances are (though few figures are available to support this) that a brief look is enough to satisfy 98 per cent of the people who want to see the Grand Canyon. Most would scarcely mind the jostling crowds in any case; available figures suggest that many visitors like the national parks *because* there are plenty of people about.

A brief look, nevertheless, is hardly a thorough understanding. And if millions cannot be accommodated on the river, along the trails, or in the air, how then can they fully enjoy the park which their taxes are supporting?

Environmental and social scientists are already studying ways to give many people a satisfying experience in the national parks; can such an experience be gained at the Grand Canyon without a visitor's having to enter the Canyon itself?

There is one method, for example, that would show a visitor who does not care to leave the rim more than he could see from the air, more than on a mule trip (without the rigors of the saddle), more than on a hike, and more variety than on a dozen tramways.

In an audiovisual age there should be no difficulty in planning and producing a series of motion pictures that would bring the Canyon to life and color for millions who will never get into it. The current capacity of this medium to capture reality is so effective that in the future such films should be overwhelming.

By whatever means—Cinerama, multiple screen, or Super-70—the walls of a projection chamber could come alive with form and color and movement, and the air vibrate with faithful reproductions of the sounds of birds, the thunder of storms, the singing of wind in the pines. Men of vision, through film, could open and enlarge the minds of visitors to the enormous range of the Canyon's unforgettable wonders.

Such a method could be regarded as a poor substitute for the real thing, and be dismissed contemptuously as a celluloid wilderness. But a good film is more than celluloid, just as a book is more than paper, a painting more than canvas, or music more than the strings and keys of instruments.

Our experience suggests that even though many people prefer the solitude, most would rather enjoy the wilderness without the sweat of the trail, the heat, the sore muscles. Such persons would be likely to support preservation efforts if they could be encouraged to understand the natural scene without having to enter it.

Unhappy as that suggestion seems, the simple fact is that the Grand Canyon, big as it is, will not be big enough to hold all human beings who may some day wish to enter it. If we do not, therefore, find other ways to show American citizens their heritage without each person having to subject himself to contact with it and perhaps to hardships, then support for wilderness preservation could conceivably diminish. The uninformed could continue to equate "wilderness" with "wasteland"—something to develop, populate, and industrialize.

One introductory film at the Grand Canyon, for example, could present a day in the life of a tassel-eared squirrel, revealing facets of the south rim forest that few human beings have time to discover even if they go there.

Another film could "fly" the audience over the Canyon from one end to the other, at dawn, at midday, at sunset, taking the passengers down past yellow ledges, over amphitheaters, across low platforms, and into the inner gorge. That type of thing has already been done in commercial Cinerama with telling effect. The audience would see natural bridges, sunless narrows, inaccessible Indian ruins, hidden waterfalls—a whole new vision of the canyon's vast immensity and continuity. The inspired visitor who then went to the rim could thrill to the view without interruptions by the sound of aircraft engines.

In another chamber visitors could take a cinema hike down any of several trails, explore old mines, cool off at a spring, watch night arrive, and see the moon break out in a sweep of mellow light across the cliffs. They might explore familiar sights, such as Ribbon Falls and Roaring Springs, and then the unfamiliar, such as Thunder River

A hidden fall in Elves Chasm.

(the roar would be unforgettable), Kanab Creek Canyon, and the historic diggings on Horseshoe Mesa.

On the way they might see a band of coyotes and hear their howls, or listen to the delicate songs of a flight of larks. They could sit beside a water hole and see what animals come to drink. They could watch the clouds play in and out of the gorge, with perhaps a time-lapse scene to show action imperceptible to human eyes without a camera. They could visit Cheyava Falls when the Redwall cliff was covered with ice. Or camp around a fire, hike to a lonely pool, watch the progression of beavers, foxes, bighorns and all the rest.

Care would be essential not to go too far, nor abrogate the simple responsibility of dignity, nor add what nature didn't put there. To condense the experience would be the idea, but without a feeling of artificiality.

In another chamber, viewers could take the trail to Havasu Canyon, revel in the beauty of the redbud tree and know the fleeting moments of perfection in spring, or the rich red color of prickly pear fruits in their autumn prime. They could come to know the habits and happiness of the Havasupai Indians, their language, their dances, their horsemanship, their festivals, and even their trials and tribulations. They could see and hear the waterfalls, see the orchids beside the pools or the mimulus and maidenhair fern at a spring. All the music would be there. All the color. All the inspiration.

And this would make that hot and dusty horseback trip unnecessary for future travelers whose presence might overload and destroy the fragile beauty of Havasu Canyon. Or who would contribute further to destruction of the Havasupai way of life.

Half a dozen such films might satisfy the yearnings of most newcomers to the Canyon. At Colonial Williamsburg, two projection chambers in constant operation present a professional film that captures the spirit of the colonial period and conveys it with elegance, dignity, and realism.

Such a technique obviously would be no substitute for the real thing. "How useless is painting," Pascal has said, "which attracts admiration of things, the originals of which we do not admire!" And yet, by contradiction, we are going to need some kind of substitute at the Grand Canyon, or the real thing will be destroyed. Perhaps it is time to depart from the time-honored notion that pictures cannot do justice to the Canyon. Though pictures cannot convey all the

194

Colorado River at Hance Rapids.

thrill of discovery or sense of depth (which a short visit to the rim would do), they can show far more than our eyes perceive.

Such films would take many months, or years, to produce, if they were to do justice to the Canyon. They would require sensitive experienced professional crews outside of government. The cost could run into millions of dollars if they were to capture coyotes calling, waterfalls clinging to cliffs as tons of ice, howling dust storms, roaring floods—all episodes relatively rare.

A program about the river could show every aspect of running the rapids, camping on sand bars, floating through paradise gorges, exploring side canyons, and examining the fascinating manifestations of inner canyon plant and animal life.

Under these circumstances, it might be some relief to a potential river runner to know what the trip was like, or blunt the pain of his not being able to get a ticket for one of the limited number of river trips permitted in future years.

And if the urge to run the Colorado River remained, then other opportunities upstream could be explored—for instance, raft trips on the San Juan, Green, Yampa, or upper Colorado outside the national park. It is not as if the Grand Canyon were the only place to engage in these activities.

Similarly, impulsive hikers unable to get an immediate quota allotment to hike in the inner gorge, could obtain temporary relief by hiking through any of a thousand other southwestern canyons.

How successful such film programs would be is open to question. They would be a good substitute for flying over the Canyon, less so for hiking within it. But something is needed to serve the millions of owners (the general public) who support the preservation of the Grand Canyon and feel that they have a right at least to see it, to understand it, to be proud of it; something that, unhappy as any solution may have to be, will keep great numbers of people from spilling into the interior of the Canyon proper or flying over it in order to enjoy it. If something isn't done, it may someday be necessary to allocate visits on the basis of how many the Canyon can take. If films do not work, something else must.

For visitors who will be inspired by the films, or who will not be pleased with less than the real thing, let them hike in, camp, explore, or run the river—in properly limited numbers. Perhaps the old trails could be rehabilitated and permits distributed on the basis of hiking competence, popularity of each trail, and so on. But it seems inevitable that, unless the population decreases or public demand diminishes, we shall have to have, strange as it sounds, a controlled-access canyon.

And that would be a sad result of excessive multiplication of human beings and their insufficiently restrained activities. If human populations could be controlled, not only in number but in behavior as well, there might never have to be either celluloid alternatives or unpleasant restrictions to a visit to the Grand Canyon. But in any case, the Canyon and wildlife must prevail.

Dr. Raymond Dasmann, the well-known specialist in environmental conservation, went straight to the heart of the matter when irritated by comments calling for removal of bears from national parks because bears were dangerous to people.

"Some of us," he said, "are of the opinion that our national parks were set aside to preserve unique and irreplaceable natural environments, and that since bears are an integral part of such environments, parks are for bears. Where people conflict with the goal of preservation of these unique natural environments people must be excluded."

14

WANDERING

"IT IS NOT the eighth wonder of the world but the first," said John C. Van Dyke.

Today a great many people of that world are observing very carefully what the United States—which by chance owns this first wonder—does with it.

No national park in the country is better known internationally than the Grand Canyon, and public land administrators in other lands are watching how the people of the United States resolve their conflicts of humanity and technology versus the national parks. Similar conflicts are developing within nearly every other nation.

"We are impressed by the statement embodied in the national parks act of 1916," said Zafar Futehally, a distinguished Indian conservationist who visited the Grand Canyon in 1967. "This has a lesson for our own countries."

A hundred other countries have national park systems, with little time or money to waste in experimentation on how to manage them. The heads of those park systems do not necessarily want to adopt the American way of doing things, nor should they, but they benefit enormously from mistakes made and corrected in North America—and they know it. After that they can exercise their own inalienable right to err.

Some do. The Amazon is being efficiently exploited. Its animals are being shipped away by air on a scale that parallels the elimination of bison from western North America. Were railroads to enter the tropical forests, the end could be near for toucans, parrots, and monkeys so often sold in pet stores, and for jaguars whose hides are sought for coats. Likewise, a number of native tribes are being reduced to second-class citizens simply because they cannot compete with the incoming hordes of settlers. It is the American West all over again.

Africans feel the pressure for additional grazing and farming lands, so encroachments against wild lands increase, slowed only by tourism and its handsome earnings of foreign exchange.

New Zealand allows aircraft to land on glaciers of Mount Cook National Park. Thailand has a golf course in Khao Yai National Park. Other places have large commercial ski developments or ugly tramways. These do not entirely overwhelm the purposes for which the parks were set aside, but they are unpleasant precedents and are certainly headaches to manage.

Fortunately, public attitudes are shifting in other countries. What were once extolled as valuable gimmicks for tourists are now deemed disadvantages that distract from the beauty and solitude of national parks. Some countries have more restrictive policies than those in effect in the United States, and as a result are approaching more rapidly the ideal international view of what a national park should be.

Swiss National Park, for example, contains deep valleys and high peaks in the heart of the Alps. The park is regarded as a field laboratory; tourists enter but do not remain, and are restricted to certain trails. Yet they learn a great deal from the unique animal relationships that can be observed. All research on the natural history of the park is systematically coordinated by the Swiss Academy of Sciences, and results are published in memoirs.

As a result of the restrictions and protection, deer and chamois have replaced sheep and cattle that used to graze on the slopes. The balance between animals and habitat has been restored, and vegetation is recovering.

It is thus becoming clear that an ecosystem cannot be managed for a "certain purpose" any more than it can be managed for a "multiple purpose." An ecosystem has marvelous powers of sustenance and recovery, but when tampered with it simply ceases to be what it was. 199

The French, as always, have a word for it. A park will be natural, they say, or it will not be.

Each ecosystem has many variables, as a computer system has. Indeed, man might be able to program the management of an ecosystem if he were able to measure the elements of which it is composed and feed them into a machine. Work of such a nature has already begun, but knowledge may have to come slowly. Man knows too little about ecosystems to expect immediate competence in managing them correctly.

Nevertheless, environmental management and applied ecology are now fundamental concepts by which the national parks are managed. The objective is to maintain the natural integrity of biotic associations.

For all its troubles—at least its present and foreseeable troubles—the Grand Canyon still possesses a great deal of its original mystery and grandeur. With the foresight of such men as Theodore Roosevelt, and the concerted efforts of the National Park Service for more than half a century, the Grand Canyon retains a great deal of its wilderness spell.

The Abert squirrel still leaps through the forest like a rolling wave, and dines on twigs of yellow pine.

The north rim blooms like a mountain garden, where deer still wander on rolling meadows and the wild Calypso opens its color in a sunlit glade.

The sun still sets with a splash of splendor on Point Sublime, the road to which is as rough and rugged as it always was.

The wind sweeps up through Angel's Window and sifts through pines at the Canyon's edge, making them sing like violins and dance in the dusky light.

At Cheyava Falls the ice still forms on winter nights and meets the day with a dazzling glaze of reflected suns. And on the trail to get there, one may witness, if the weather is right, a frenzied race of shadows from flying clouds. Or, come winter, one may see snow flurries run after each other across the blackbrush flats.

The redbud blooms in Supai yet and summer storms roar over the rim of Transept Canyon. Rainbows shine through veils of mist or curve in arcs that fall beneath the rim.

The memory of Clarence Dutton lingers over the north rim forest as well as the volcanic valleys of Toroweap. The spirit of Powell pervades the river regions.

200

Yesterday's miracles are almost all on display. As William Hamilton Nelson once wrote: "Hopi Indians say Grand Canyon is an entrance to Heaven, and all we can say is that they have a wonderful sense of location."

George Wharton James, who explored this canyon at the turn of the century, learned from the lessons of the wind:

Sand soon anchors and buries the rolling tumbleweed.

There is an abiding sense of the presence of the Almighty, all-powerful, all-loving, all-merciful, that soothes and hushes and quiets the distressed and wounded soul, so that a normal equilibrium is gained and strength restored to return to one's place, manfully to fight one's true battles with the world, the flesh, and the devil. To me this Canyon is the Holy of Holies, the Inner Temple, where each man may be his own High Priest, open the sacred veil, and stand face to face with the Divine. And he who can thus "talk with God" may not show it to his fellows, but he knows within himself the new power, calmness, and equanimity which he has gained, and he returns to life's struggles thankful for these glimpses of the Divine.

And what of the thoughts of a man who studied the Canyon for more than twenty years? Louis Schellbach, long-time park naturalist, never tired of it. We used to sit by the hour and listen to him tell how the Canyon helped to develop human perception.

"The lower animals cannot do these things," he said. "We can think that two and two are four. We think of the distance to the stars. We enjoy the sunset. No other living creature can do this. Then why not develop our senses so that we can enjoy just the sheer love of life? The enjoyment of living?"

Louis would ask the visitors in his audiences why they were rushing through life. Then he would exhort them to linger along the way as they traveled, and to enjoy the songs of life.

It is easy to exist, he would say, but to enjoy life involves understanding some of its intangibles. "That way," he added, "even when you are alone you are never lonely. Life is an adventure that we are sharing briefly with other creatures—very briefly. Let us enjoy it to the fullest."

He maintained that the view from the rim of the Canyon could make a man or woman realize how foolish was our hectic human pace. "Time is a man-made tool," he would say. "Man invented time, so as to get a concept of duration, of what went before and what came after an event. As far as nature is concerned, there is no such thing as time.

"What do you mean by time? There is Paleozoic time, Archaic time, moon time, solar time, cosmic time, Carbon 14 time, overtime, supper time, anytime—until this has become man's master. It is a good tool. But it is not a good master."

The Grand Canyon will always, God and the public willing,

Among the fir and aspen at Vista Encantada.

202

remain a source of contentment, inspiration, and humility for man-
kind. As a spot for reconditioning the human spirit, it is unexcelled.
Men now have begun to realize that they must be obedient to universal laws over which they lack control.

Grand Canyon National Park is still not large enough, but 26,000
acres of Marble Canyon, including 50 miles of the Colorado River,
were added in 1969. That helps.

And just in time, for all indications are that the seventies will be
the most expansive era yet in business. The standard of living is
expected to increase 40 per cent, and the average salary by about
the same. Barring major disaster, productivity and growth will make
the national parks increasingly attractive.

The National Park Service expects more than three million visits
annually to the Grand Canyon by 1978.

And by 1998?

Until the law is amended, we can still provide a system whereby
millions of people are permitted a look at this great scenic wonder,
and perhaps a chance to get off by themselves for a while. A look
or two is likely to be all most visitors, and most potential visitors,
want, providing they see a fairly pristine natural scene.

Dr. Stanley A. Cain, the distinguished ecologist and onetime
Assistant Secretary of the Interior, once said:

The great parks cannot be protected for the pleasures that people take
in their natural values if we administrators respond to every demand
made by the public. It is all too easy to measure "success" by counting
visitors and to respond to demands by adding some development here
and some more there until what was sought to be preserved has been
irrevocably lost. There is a saturation point beyond which the wilderness experience cannot be had, beyond which a campground is no
longer a pleasant place. Parks need to apply the familiar rangeland
concept of carrying capacity. Innumerable people cannot enjoy solitude
together.

204 If we continue to make Grand Canyon wilder than it was thirty
or forty years ago—as is being done in such places as Yosemite
National Park in California—it will be a more wonderful, quiet,
impressive, and memorable experience. We will have eliminated
the irony of travelers who come twelve thousand miles to enjoy the
Canyon and find it full of noise and aircraft.

In so doing, we shall have fulfilled the mandate of Congress and
resolved the conflicts inherent in it. We shall have conserved the
scenery and the wildlife, and provided for human pleasure and

inspiration in a manner that will leave the Canyon unimpaired for the enjoyment of future generations.

The Canyon is needed for that uncounted number of people for whom one look is enough to change a life or produce a fresh respect for country, a new appreciation of nature, and perhaps a profound understanding of creation.

It is needed by those who know how to go into and come out again without leaving more than a footprint behind, and who draw immense renewal from being enveloped within its beauty and solitude.

To all of them this is a place for wandering, a place to walk, to wonder, to think, to believe. It is part of a universal message that has been around for a very long time: Enjoy to the fullest the adventure of life.

Appendix 1.

Hiking in the Grand Canyon

For advance planning, full and up-to-date information on trail conditions, regulations, emergency measures, weather, and hiker require-
ments is available on request to: The Superintendent, Grand Canyon
National Park, Grand Canyon, Arizona, 86023. In addition, topographic maps of the United States Geological Survey show a number
of trails, and these should be carefully examined ahead of time; hikers
should keep maps pertaining to the route in their packs at all times.
Maps of *Grand Canyon National Park*, plus *Grand Canyon National
Monument*, give all-inclusive coverage. For closer detail of the rims
as well as the inner canyon, the following United States Geological
Survey quadrangles, all in Arizona, should be consulted: *Grandview
Point, Vishnu Temple, Nankoweap, Bright Angel, De Motte Park,
Havasupai Point, Powell Plateau, Supai, Kanab Point, National Can-
yon,* and *Tuckup Canyon.*

Such maps are available from local map sales offices or directly from
the following sales offices of the United States Geological Survey:

Distribution Section, Geological Survey, Federal Center
Denver, Colorado 80225.

Distribution Section, Geological Survey
1200 South Eads Street, Arlington, Virginia 22202.

Even after the most careful planning, it is essential—and required
by park regulations—to check in at the district ranger's office before
traveling on any nonmaintained route. Nature occasionally alters the
Canyon without prior notice, and rangers have the responsibility for
rescuing hikers in trouble. In case of an accident, it eases their job

enormously to know where a hiker was heading, when and by what route he intended to get there, and when he expected to return. That basic information could narrow the circle of search from more than a thousand square miles to less than ten, and could enable rescuers to reach him in time to save his life. The margin for error in this Canyon is not very wide.

A. TRAILS

Bright Angel Trail. South rim to river, eight miles. Upper terminus at Grand Canyon Village. Vertical descent, 4,500 feet. Well maintained, safe, and heavily used by both men and mules. This trail has water, rest rooms, emergency telephones, and camping and picnic sites, the only south-rim trail to be so fully supplied. Trailside labels explain features of interest along the way.

Kaibab Trail. North rim to south rim, twenty-one miles. Scenic and spectacular. Connects Bright Angel Point on the north rim with Yaki Point on the south rim, via Phantom Ranch and the Kaibab suspension bridge across the Colorado River. Safe and well maintained, but subject to rare disastrous floods that render portions of it, particularly the north section along Bright Angel Creek, unusable for long periods. Heaviest flood damage generally occurs in winter or spring, but sudden summer cloudbursts can wreak havoc. This is the main cross-Canyon route, and one of the most delightful hikes in the Southwest. An exhibit of fossil ferns has been installed on the South Kaibab portion, and trail labels explain other features of interest. Water is available on the north section but not on the south.

River Trail. A 1.8-mile riverside route connecting the foot of Bright Angel Trail with the Kaibab Trail. Safe and well maintained, this trail affords splendid views of the Colorado River and occasional access to the water's edge. Descending the South Kaibab Trail from Yaki Point, then hiking down river on this trail and ascending the Bright Angel Trail to Grand Canyon Village makes a splendid two-day circle route. Some hardy hikers do it in a day, and we knew an African game warden who did it in an afternoon, but such endurance tests in this canyon are, for 99 per cent of us, foolhardy and dangerous.

Hermit Trail. The best of the abandoned trails from the standpoint of trail condition. Seven miles from the south rim near Hermit's Rest to the old abandoned Hermit Camp on the Tonto Platform below, with an additional clamber through mesquite along Hermit Creek to the Colorado River. Tricky footing in places due to landslides and loose rocks. Water is available. The National Park Service says this is a good introduction to wilderness hiking in the Canyon and recommends that the trip down and out cover two days.

Waldron Trail. In Hermit Basin, fair condition only, 1½ miles. A pleasant, easy-to-follow trail that connects the Hermit Trail in Hermit Basin with Horsethief Tank on the south rim. The trail is well defined and has good switchbacks all the way to the rim.

Tanner Trail. South rim to river, twelve miles. Longest, driest, and hottest of the rim-to-river routes. Not impassable, but often vague and in places missing. A rigorous challenge and a long trip requiring plenty of time, water, and stamina.

Grandview Trail. Rough, waterless, but popular three-mile trail from Grandview Point to Horseshoe Mesa, where early mining operations were once carried on. Mine shafts, now in disrepair and dangerous, should not be entered. From Horseshoe Mesa three unmarked trails lead down to the Tonto Trail but not to the river. Water is available, but the hiker must know where to look, which is a foremost reason for getting advance information from park headquarters.

Hance Trail (Red Canyon). Eight-mile trail from the south rim, near Moran Point, to the Colorado River. The dry, erratic, badly disintegrating, route is vague and illogical, leading to confusion and delays, which need to be allowed for when programming time and water in advance.

Old Hance Trail (Hance Canyon). The National Park Service advises against the use of this trail, which is old and ruined, dangerous and lacking in scenic appeal. They recommend other ways of getting into Hance Canyon.

Louis Boucher (Silver Bell) Trail. From rim to river and back on this route, twenty-two miles. Much of the trip involves going from one landmark to another, with progress often slow and difficult. Coming back out via the Tonto and Hermit Trails may be easier and has the advantage of making it a circular route. Some permanent water is available. The Boucher Trail should not be ascended unless the hiker is confident that he knows the way up.

Bass Trail. Far to the west of Grand Canyon Village, this trail leaves the rim and descends nine miles to the Colorado River. There are many boulders, places where switchbacks have been washed out, and portions overgrown with brush. There is no reliable source of water. Still, it is a historic trip, recalling the early mining attempts within the Canyon.

Tonto Trail. This entire trail is within the Canyon, and is one of the few that trends primarily east and west. One end lies in Garnet Canyon on the west, and the other at Red Canyon, below Moran Point on the east. The distance between—approximately seventy-five miles by trail—extends principally over the Tonto Platform, an open, arid, inner-canyon plateau that offers splendid views but difficult hiking and not many dependable sources of water. Burro trails often lead the unobservant hiker astray. Nevertheless, the Tonto Trail offers connections

209

with other trails that afford variation in selection of routes for hiking trips.

Hualapai Trail. An easy eight-mile trail into Havasu Canyon from the south. Once at the village of the Havasupai Indians, a hiker must travel another two to four miles of trail to reach the famous waterfalls along Havasu Creek, and another five miles to reach the Colorado River. The lower trail is varied, wet, sometimes difficult, sometimes hand-over-hand down a cliff, but altogether a delightful challenge because of the water and the beauty of the canyon.

Topocoba Trail. This trail also leads into Havasu Canyon, but is much longer than the Hualapai Trail. From rim to village, a hiker must cover a fourteen-mile trip on which there is no drinking water.

Clear Creek Trail. Connects Bright Angel Creek, near Phantom Ranch, with Clear Creek, a distance of about nine miles. Spectacular views but no water. The trail is in fair condition to Clear Creek, but if a hiker wants to get to Cheyava Falls, he is virtually on his own in finding a way upstream.

Old North Kaibab Trail. A delightful seven-mile route from the north rim to Roaring Springs. Care and a good map, plus directions from park rangers, will facilitate use of this route. Like all abandoned trails, it is either grown over in places or washed out, or both, but in this case water exists. At the bottom of the trail a hiker may either go on across the Canyon or return to the north rim via the present-day Kaibab Trail, which is well maintained.

Shinumo Trail (North Bass Trail). Connects the Colorado River with Swamp Point, on the north rim, a distance of fourteen miles. This is a northward extension of the old Bass Trail. Care is required in finding the way and considerable energy may be expended in getting through vegetation that has grown over the trail, but withal it is an exciting trip.

Thunder River Trail. Thirteen miles of waterless trail leading from a place called Indian Hollow, north of the north rim of the Grand Canyon, to Thunder River. The roar of the river and sight of the plunging cataracts of Thunder Spring are breathtaking. The river pours into Tapeats Creek very promptly, and it is possible for a hiker to make his way down that creek to the Colorado River. All this provides a thrilling wilderness experience, but it is so far from civilization, and hence so far from help, that all prospective hikers should check in with park rangers on the north rim and go well equipped.

Nankoweap Trail connects Saddle Mountain, on the north rim near Point Imperial, with the Colorado River in the eastern portion of the Canyon, twelve miles. A long, dry hike with tricky and difficult going in places, requiring more than ordinary care, but the trail passes through some of the most spectacular scenery in the Grand Canyon.

Toroweap Trail. Also known as Lava Falls Trail. A steep, rugged

1½ miles from Vulcan's Throne, in Grand Canyon National Monument, down a lava cascade to the Colorado River. No constructed trail, merely a "way to go," which is delineated by rock monuments at intervals along the way. The route offers treacherous footing where it passes over cinders and loose rocks. There is no water except at the river. Average hiking time: two hours down and four hours up.

Tuckup Trail. Also called Tuweep Trail in the past. A sixty-four mile trail from lower Toroweap Valley to Boysag Point. Trail is ill defined in places but still passable, even to horses. Several springs exist along the way, but only Schmutz, June (Willow), and Cottonwood are dependable; these have a high lime content but are usable. Hiking is slow on account of many zigzags and ups and downs.

Self-guiding Trails. At several places along both rims, park naturalists have laid out interesting routes through the forest. In some cases, signs along the way serve as labels in an outdoor museum. In others numbered stakes beside the trail correspond to numbered paragraphs in folders, which describe the trees and shrubs, fossils, rocks, and other features of the natural scene. Inquire at park information offices regarding the location of these trails.

B. REGULATIONS AND SUGGESTIONS

1. The National Park Service requires that all persons intending to hike on a nonmaintained trail register at a ranger station. Equipment and supplies must be inspected by park rangers. All hikers must be physically competent to complete the projected trip.

2. Use only regularly established campgrounds where available. Take your own fuel, *i.e.*, charcoal or gas stove.

3. A fire permit is required for camping away from established campgrounds.

4. Do not hike alone on nonmaintained trails.

5. Destruction, defacement, removal, or disturbance of park features or property is prohibited. This includes all vegetation, all animal life, every form of rock, mineral, or fossil, every prehistoric ruin or artifact, and every modern structure installed for the safety, convenience, and education of park visitors.

6. Leave the park in a better condition than you found it. Carry all litter to the nearest trash can or pack it back to the rim.

7. Dogs and cats are prohibited on trails within the canyon.

8. Bicycles and motorized vehicles are prohibited on all park trails.

9. Rolling or throwing of rocks and other objects off the trails, ledges, or rims is strictly forbidden.

10. Avoid taking short cuts, especially across switchbacks.

11. If injured, stay where you are. Searchers will be out looking if you are twenty-four hours overdue.

12. When lost, try to retrace your steps to the last known point on the trail. If that is impossible, stop and await a search party.

13. In an emergency, three fires or flares, three shouts, three of anything is the signal for distress.

14. When meeting mules or horses, either in pack trains or tourist passenger strings, do as requested by the leader of the mounted party. Generally, a hiker should stand quietly on the outside of the trail and make no sudden movements or noises while trail animals are in the vicinity.

15. Report to park rangers upon completion of any trip over non-maintained trails.

16. No one should venture down any of the old trails without first traveling a similar distance on one of the used, maintained trails, the Bright Angel or Kaibab.

17. Carry sufficient water, normally one gallon per man per day.

18. Beware of prolonged exposure to the sun, or to intense heat.

19. On trails with uncertain footing remember that your pack helps to throw you off balance.

C. WHAT TO WEAR AND CARRY

The following list contains the basic essentials for a safe and reasonably comfortable Canyon hike, depending on how Spartan a hiker wishes to be. More experienced hikers have their own preferences, but the average person who does rugged hiking only occasionally may wish to check his equipment and clothing against this list and decide for himself what he needs.

Sun hat
Long-sleeved shirt
Good quality boots with rubber gripper soles and heels
Comfortable socks
Warm clothes in winter
Long trousers or walking shorts, as desired
Water in canteen
Lightweight foods (raisins, nonmelting chocolate, etc.)
Matches
Snakebite kit
First-aid kit
Extra small bandages
Signal mirror
Flashlight

Maps
Compass
Water-purification tablets
Extra socks, handkerchiefs, shirts, etc.
Comfortable pack with good shoulder straps
Sunburn remedy
Toilet paper
Sleeping bag, small stove, and fuel if on long trip
Sunglasses
Binoculars
Camera, exposure meter, film
Swim suit

D. THE PROBLEM OF WATER

Above everything else that governs the entry of man into the Grand Canyon's wilderness is the availability of water. The trails are long and often arduous; their remoteness and difficulty insulate a hiker from help. The Canyon's depths confine him like a roofless cage. Therefore the success of his survival depends on access to potable water.

Springs abound, but they are often hard to see or find. Their locations as shown on maps may be difficult to pinpoint on the ground if rock slides have come down around them. They may be dry. They may be polluted—if not by man and horses, then by wild burros. They may be poisonous; an eminent scientist once became severely ill by drinking from a source of bad water in this Canyon.

The water in clear tributaries running into the Colorado River is usually pure—except for the one most persons visit. Thanks to domestic stock fording Bright Angel Creek up the North Kaibab Trail, the National Park Service has to discourage drinking of water from that most delightful—and originally well named—of streams. Bright Angel Creek is polluted. Even Havasu Creek has become contaminated.

The Colorado River itself should normally be above acceptable levels of potability. If muddy, the suspended sediments need about twenty minutes to settle, after which the clear water can be removed. However, with increasing uses upstream and burgeoning river travel, the degree of pollution will need to be watched in the years ahead.

Appendix 2.

An Act to Establish the Grand Canyon National Park in the State of Arizona, approved February 26, 1919 (40 Stat. 1175)

Be it enacted by the Senate and House of Representatives of the United States of America in Congress assembled, That there is hereby reserved and withdrawn from settlement, occupancy, or disposal under the laws of the United States and dedicated and set apart as a public park for the benefit and enjoyment of the people, under the name of the "Grand Canyon National Park," the tract of land in the State of Arizona particularly described by and included within metes and bounds as follows, to wit: . . .

Sec. 2. That the administration, protection, and promotion of said Grand Canyon National Park shall be exercised, under the direction of the Secretary of the Interior, by the National Park Service, subject to the provisions of the Act of August twenty-fifth, nineteen hundred and sixteen, entitled "An Act to establish a National Park Service, and for other purposes": *Provided,* That all concessions for hotels, camps, transportation, and other privileges of every kind and nature for the accommodation or entertainment of visitors shall be let at public bidding to the best and most responsible bidder.

Sec. 3. That nothing herein contained shall affect the rights of the Havasupai Tribe of Indians to the use and occupancy of the bottom lands of the Canyon of Cataract Creek as described in the Executive order of March thirty-first, eighteen hundred and eighty-two, and the Secretary of the Interior is hereby authorized, in his discretion, to permit individual members of said tribe to use and occupy other tracts of land within said park for agricultural purposes.

Sec. 4. That nothing herein contained shall affect any valid existing claim, location, or entry under the land laws of the United States, whether for homestead, mineral, right of way, or any other purpose whatsoever, or shall affect the rights of any such claimant, locator, or entryman to the full use and enjoyment of his land and nothing herein contained shall affect, diminish, or impair the right and authority of the county of Coconino, in the State of Arizona, to levy and collect tolls for the passage of livestock over and upon the Bright Angel Toll Road and Trail, and the Secretary of the Interior is hereby authorized to negotiate with the said county of Coconino for the purchase of said Bright Angel Toll Road and Trail and all rights therein, and report to Congress at as early a date as possible the terms upon which the property can be procured.

Sec. 5. That whenever consistent with the primary purposes of said park the Act of February fifteenth, nineteen hundred and one, applicable to the locations of rights of way in certain national parks and the national forests for irrigation and other purposes, and subsequent Acts shall be and remain applicable to the lands included within the park. The Secretary of the Interior may, in his discretion and upon such conditions as he may deem proper, grant easements or rights of way for railroads upon or across the park.

Sec. 6. That whenever consistent with the primary purposes of said park, the Secretary of the Interior is authorized, under general regulations to be prescribed by him, to permit the prospecting, development, and utilization of the mineral resources of said park upon such terms and for specified periods, or otherwise, as he may deem to be for the best interests of the United States.

Sec. 7. That, whenever consistent with the primary purposes of said park, the Secretary of the Interior is authorized to permit the utilization of areas therein which may be necessary for the development and maintenance of a Government reclamation project.

Sec. 8. That where privately owned lands within the said park lie within three hundred feet of the rim of the Grand Canyon no building, tent, fence, or other structure shall be erected on the park lands lying between said privately owned lands and the rim.

216   Sec. 9. The Executive order of January eleventh, nineteen hundred and eight, creating the Grand Canyon National Monument, is hereby revoked and repealed, and such parts of the Grand Canyon National Game Preserve, designated under authority of the Act of Congress, approved June twenty-ninth, nineteen hundred and six, entitled "An Act for the protection of wild animals in the Grand Canyon Forest Reserve," as are by this Act included with the Grand Canyon National Park are hereby excluded and eliminated from said game preserve.

Appendix 3.

Address by President Theodore Roosevelt at Grand Canyon, Arizona, May 6, 1903.

Mr. Governor, and you, my Fellow-Citizens:

I am glad to be in Arizona to-day. From Arizona many gallant men came into the regiment which I had the honor to command. Arizona sent men who won glory on fought fields, and men to whom came a glorious and an honorable death fighting for the flag of their country. As long as I live it will be to me an inspiration to have served with Bucky O'Neill. I have met so many comrades whom I prize, for whom I feel respect and admiration and affection, that I shall not particularize among them except to say that there is none for whom I feel all of respect and admiration and affection more than for your Governor.

I have never been in Arizona before. It is one of the regions from which I expect most development through the wise action of the National Congress in passing the irrigation act. The first and biggest experiment now in view under that act is the one that we are trying in Arizona. I look forward to the effects of irrigation partly as applied by and through the government, still more as applied by individuals, and especially by associations of individuals, profiting by the example of the government, and possibly by help from it—I look forward to the effects of irrigation as being of greater consequence to all this region of country in the next fifty years than any other material movement whatsoever.

In the Grand Canyon, Arizona has a natural wonder which, so far as I know, is in kind absolutely unparalleled throughout the rest of the world. I want to ask you to do one thing in connection with it in your own interest and in the interest of the country—to keep this great wonder of nature as it now is. I was delighted to learn of the wisdom of the Santa Fe railroad people in deciding not to build their hotel on the brink of the canyon. I hope you will not have a building of any kind, not a summer cottage, a hotel, or anything else, to mar the wonderful grandeur, the sublimity, the great loneliness and beauty of the canyon. Leave it as it is. You can not improve on it. The ages have been at work on it, and man can only mar it. What you can do is to keep it for your children, your children's children, and for all who come after you, as one of the great sights which every American if he can travel at all should see. We have gotten past the stage, my fellow-citizens, when we are to be pardoned if we treat any part of our country as something to be skinned for two or three years for the use of the present generation, whether it is for the forest, the water, the scenery. Whatever it is, handle it so that your children's children will get the benefit of it. If you deal with irrigation, apply it under circumstances that will make it of benefit, not to the speculator who hopes to get profit out of it for two or three years, but handle it so that it will be of use to the home-maker, to the man who comes to live here, and to have his children stay after him. Keep the forest in the same way. Preserve the forests by use; preserve them for the ranchman and the stockman, for the people of the Territory, for the people of the region round about. Preserve them for that use, but use them so that they will not be squandered, that they will not be wasted, so that they will be of benefit to the Arizona of 1953 as well as the Arizona of 1903.

To the Indians here I want to say a word of welcome. In my regiment I had a good many Indians. They were good enough to fight and to die, and they are good enough to have me treat them exactly as squarely as any white man. There are many problems in connection with them. We must save them from corruption and from brutality; and I regret to say that at times we must save them from unregulated Eastern philanthropy. All I ask is a square deal for every man. Give him a fair chance. Do not let him wrong any one, and do not let him be wronged.

I believe in you. I am glad to see you. I wish you well with all my heart, and I know that your future will justify all the hopes we have.

Appendix 4.

The Sublimest Thing on Earth

Excerpts from the writings of Clarence E. Dutton

"In no other portion of the world are the natural laws governing the processes of land sculpture exemplified so grandly; nowhere else are their results set forth so clearly. The interest excited by the grandeur of the subjects is intensified, and the value of the lessons enhanced, by the exceptionally intelligible manner in which their materials are presented for study."

So wrote a man who for ten years, between 1875 and 1885, roamed the plateau country, endured its heat, thirsted in its dryness, climbed its rugged trails, and reveled in the solitude and magnificence of the land. Clarence E. Dutton (1841–1912), Connecticut-born and a graduate of Yale, was an army ordnance officer and geologist assigned on special detail to the Powell Survey. He wrote some of the best descriptions ever to have come from the Grand Canyon region, and we present here an excerpt from his writings. The selection is arbitrary because he wrote so much that was superb, but it shows his style and gives an idea of his insights, which now seem timeless. This selection, from The Physical Geology of the Grand Cañon District, *published in 1882, is Dutton's description of the Grand Canyon as seen upon arrival at the north rim after a journey through the dense Kaibab forest.*

Wherever we reach the Grand Cañon in the Kaibab it bursts upon the vision in a moment. Seldom is any warning given that we are near the brink. At the Toroweap it is quite otherwise. There we are notified that we are near it a day before we reach it. As the final march to that portion of the chasm is made the scene gradually develops, growing by insensible degrees more grand until at last we stand upon the brink of the inner gorge, where all is before us. In the Kaibab the forest reaches to the sharp edge of the cliff and the pine trees shed their cones into the fathomless depths below.

If the approach is made at random, with no idea of reaching any particular point by a known route, the probabilities are that it is first seen from the rim of one of the vast amphitheaters which set back from the main chasm far into the mass of the plateau. It is to such a point which the reader has been brought in the preceding chapter. Of course there are degrees in the magnitude and power of the pictures presented, but the smallest and least powerful is tremendous and too great for comprehension. The scenery of the amphitheaters far surpasses in grandeur and nobility anything else of the kind in any other region, but it is mere by-play in comparison with the panorama displayed in the heart of the cañon. The supreme views are to be obtained at the extremities of the long promontories, which jut out between these recesses far into the gulf. Towards such a point we now direct our steps. The one we have chosen is on the whole the most commanding in the Kaibab front, though there are several others which might be regarded as very nearly equal to it, or as even more imposing in some respects. We named it *Point Sublime.*

The route is of the same character as that we have already traversed —open pine forest, with smooth and gently rolling ground. The distance from the point where we first touched the rim of the amphitheater is about five miles. Nothing is seen of the chasm until about a mile from the end we come once more upon the brink. Reaching the extreme verge the packs are cast off and sitting upon the edge we contemplate the most sublime and awe-inspiring spectacle in the world.

The Grand Cañon of the Colorado is a great innovation in modern ideas of scenery, and in our conceptions of the grandeur, beauty, and power of nature. As with all great innovations it is not to be comprehended in a day or a week, nor even in a month. It must be dwelt upon and studied, and the study must comprise the slow acquisition of the meaning and spirit of that marvelous scenery which characterizes the Plateau country, and of which the great chasm is the superlative manifestation. The study and slow mastery of the influences of that class of scenery and its full appreciation is a special culture, requiring time, patience, and long familiarity for its consummation. The lover of nature, whose perceptions have been trained in the Alps, in Italy, Germany, or New England, in the Appalachians or Cordilleras, in Scotland or Colorado, would enter this strange region with a shock, and dwell there for a time with a sense of oppression, and perhaps with horror. Whatsoever things he had learned to regard as beautiful and noble he would seldom or never see, and whatsoever he might see would appear to him as anything but beautiful and noble. Whatsoever might be bold and striking would at first seem only grotesque. The colors would be the very ones he had learned to shun as tawdry and bizarre. The tones and shades modest and tender, subdued yet rich, in which his fancy had always taken special delight, would be the ones which are conspicuously absent. But time would bring a gradual change. Some day he would suddenly become conscious that outlines which at first seemed harsh and trivial have grace and meaning; that forms which seemed grotesque are full of dignity; that magnitudes which had added enormity to coarseness have become replete with strength and even majesty; that colors which had been esteemed unrefined, immodest, and glaring, are as expressive, tender, changeful, and capacious of effects as any others. Great innovations, whether in art or literature, in science or in nature, seldom take the world by storm. They must be understood before they can be estimated, and must be cultivated before they can be understood.

It is so with the Grand Cañon. The observer who visits its commanding points with the expectation of experiencing forthwith a rapturous exaltation, an ecstacy arising from the realization of a degree of grandeur and sublimity never felt before, is doomed to disappointment. Supposing him to be but little familiar with plateau scenery, he will be simply bewildered. Must he therefore pronounce it a failure, an overpraised thing? Must he entertain a just resentment towards those who may have raised his expectations too high? The answer is that subjects which disclose their full power, meaning, and beauty as soon as they are presented to the mind have very little of those qualities to disclose. Moreover a visitor to the chasm or to any other famous scene must necessarily come there (for so is the human mind constituted) with a picture of it created by his own imagination. He reaches the spot, the conjured picture vanishes in an instant, and the place of it must be filled anew. Surely no imagination can construct out of its own material any picture having the remotest resemblance to the Grand Cañon. In truth the first step in attempting a description is to beg the reader to dismiss from his mind, so far as practicable, any preconceived notion of it.

Those who have long and carefully studied the Grand Cañon of the Colorado do not hesitate for a moment to pronounce it by far the most sublime of all earth spectacles. If its sublimity consisted only in its dimensions, it could be sufficiently set forth in a single sentence. It is more than 200 miles long, from 5 to 12 miles wide, and from 5,000 to 6,000 feet deep. There are in the world valleys which are longer and a few which are deeper. There are valleys flanked by summits loftier than the palisades of the Kaibab. Still the Grand Cañon is the sublimest thing on earth. It is so not alone by virtue of its magnitudes, but by virtue of the whole—its *ensemble*.

221

In truth, the tone and temper of the landscape are constantly varying, and the changes in its aspect are very great. It is never the same, even from day to day, or even from hour to hour. In the early morning its mood and subjective influences are usually calmer and more full of repose than at other times, but as the sun rises higher the whole scene is so changed that we cannot recall our first impressions. Every passing cloud, every change in the position of the sun recasts the whole. At sunset the pageant closes amid splendors that seem more than earthly. The direction of the full sunlight, the massing of the shadows, the manner in which the side-lights are thrown in from the clouds determine these modulations, and the sensitiveness of the picture to the slightest variations in these conditions is very wonderful. . . .

At midday the clouds begin to gather, first in fleecy flecks, then in cumuli and throw their shadows into the gulf. At once the scene changes. The slumber of the chasm is disturbed. The temples and cloisters seem to raise themselves half awake to greet the passing shadow. Their wilted, drooping, flattened faces expand into relief. The long promontories reach out from the distant wall as if to catch a moment's refreshment from the shade. The colors begin to glow; the haze loses its opaque density and becomes more tenuous. The shadows pass, and the chasm relapses into its dull sleep again. Thus through the midday hours it lies in fitful slumber, overcome by the blinding glare and withering heat, yet responsive to every fluctuation of light and shadow like a delicate organism.

As the sun moves far into the west the scene again changes, slowly and imperceptibly at first, but afterwards more rapidly. In the hot summer afternoons the sky is full of cloud-play and the deep flushes with ready answers. The banks of snowy clouds pour a flood of light sidewise into the shadows and light up the gloom of the amphitheaters and alcoves, weakening the glow of the haze and rendering visible the details of the wall faces. At length as the sun draws near the horizon the great drama of the day begins.

Throughout the afternoon the prospect has been gradually growing clearer. The haze has relaxed its steely glare and has changed to a veil of transparent blue. Slowly the myriads of details have come out and the walls are flecked with lines of minute tracery, forming a diaper of light and shade. Stronger and sharper becomes the relief of each projection. The promontories come forth from the opposite wall. The sinuous lines of stratification which once seemed meaningless, distorted, and even chaotic,· now range themselves into a true perspective of graceful curves, threading the scallop edges of the strata. The colossal buttes expand in every dimension. Their long narrow wings, which once were folded together and flattened against each other, open out, disclosing between them vast alcoves illumined with Rembrandt lights tinged with the pale refined blue of the ever-present haze. A thousand forms, hitherto unseen or obscure, start up within the abyss, and stand forth in strength and animation. All things seem to grow in beauty, power, and dimensions. What was grand before has become majestic, the majestic becomes sublime, and, ever expanding and developing, the sublime passes beyond the reach of our faculties and becomes transcendent. The colors have come back. Inherently rich and strong, though not superlative, under ordinary lights, they now begin to display an adventitious brilliancy. The western sky is all aflame. The scattered banks of cloud and wavy cirrus have caught the waning splendor, and shine with orange and crimson. Broad slant beams of yellow light, shot through the glory-rifts, fall on turret and tower, on pinnacled crest, and winding ledge, suffusing them with a radiance less fulsome, but akin to that which flames in the western clouds. The summit band is brilliant yellow; the next below is pale rose. But the grand expanse within is a deep-luminous, resplendent red. The climax has now come. The blaze of sunlight poured over an illimitable surface of growing red is flung back into the gulf, and, commingling with the blue haze, turns it into a sea of purple of most imperial hue—so rich, so strong, so pure that it makes the heart ache and the throat tighten. However vast the magnitudes, however majestic the forms, or sumptuous the decoration, it is in these kingly colors that the highest glory of the Grand Cañon is revealed.

At length the sun sinks and the colors cease to burn. The abyss lapses back into repose. But its glory mounts upward and diffuses itself in the sky above. Long streamers of rosy light, rayed out from the west, cross the firmament and converge again in the east ending in a pale rosy arch, which rises like a low aurora just above the eastern horizon. Below it is the dead gray shadow of the world. Higher and higher climbs the arch followed by the darkening pall of gray, and as it ascends it fades and disappears, leaving no color except the afterglow of the western clouds, and the lusterless red of the chasm below. Within the abyss the darkness gathers. Gradually the shades deepen and ascend, hiding the opposite wall and enveloping the great temples. For a few moments the summits of these majestic piles seem to float upon a sea of blackness, then vanish in the darkness, and, wrapped in the impenetrable mantle of the night, they await the glory of the coming dawn.

Bibliography

Bancroft, Hubert Howe. *History of Arizona and New Mexico, 1530–1888.* Facsimile of the 1889 edition. Albuquerque, N.M.: Horn & Wallace, Publishers, 1962. Source book in southwestern history.

Bartlett, Richard A. *Great Surveys of the American West.* Norman, Okla.: University of Oklahoma Press, 1962. Study of Powell's and other 19th-century surveys.

Beal, Merrill D. *Grand Canyon, The Story Behind the Scenery.* Flagstaff, Ariz.: KC Publications, 1967. A park naturalist's scientific explanation.

Bolton, Herbert E. *Coronado, Knight of Pueblos and Plains.* Albuquerque, N.M.: University of New Mexico Press, 1949. Biography of the 16th-century Conquistador.

Breed, William J. *The Age of Dinosaurs in Northern Arizona.* Flagstaff, Ariz.: Museum of Northern Arizona, 1968. Brief review of life in Mesozoic times.

Corle, Edwin. *Listen, Bright Angel.* New York: Duell, Sloan and Pearce, 1946. General description and history.

Coues, Elliott. *On the Trail of a Spanish Pioneer: The Diary and Itinerary of Francisco Garcés.* New York: Francis P. Harper, 1900. Story of the 18th-century missionary priest.

Crampton, C. Gregory. *Standing Up Country: The Canyon Lands of Utah and Arizona.* New York: Alfred A. Knopf, Inc., 1964. History and natural history of the canyon country.

Darrah, William Culp. *Powell of the Colorado.* Princeton, N.J.: Princeton University Press, 1951. Biography of the famed explorer.

Darton, N.H. *Story of the Grand Canyon of Arizona: A Popular Illustrated Account of its Rocks and Origin.* Kansas City, Mo.: n.p., 1917. Pioneer geologist's account of the Canyon.

Bibliography

Day, A. Grove. *Coronado's Quest: The Discovery of the Southwestern States.* Berkeley, Calif.: University of California Press, 1964. Explorations of the Conquistadores.

Dellenbaugh, Frederick S. *A Canyon Voyage.* New York: G. P. Putnam's Sons, 1908. Down the Colorado River by boat.

——. *The Romance of the Colorado River.* Chicago: The Rio Grande Press, 1962. Early account of the Canyon region.

Dutton, Clarence E. *The Physical Geology of the Grand Cañon District.* Annual Report of the Director of the U.S. Geological Survey, 1880–1881. Washington, D.C.: Government Printing Office, 1882. Classic study by Powell Survey geologist.

Farquhar, Francis P. *The Books of the Colorado River and the Grand Canyon.* Los Angeles: Glen Dawson, 1953. Bibliography.

Fletcher, Colin. *The Man Who Walked Through Time.* New York: Alfred A. Knopf, Inc., 1967. One man's hike within Grand Canyon.

Freeman, Lewis. *The Colorado River: Yesterday, Today, and Tomorrow.* New York: Dodd, Mead, & Co., 1923. General description of the canyon country.

——. *Down the Grand Canyon.* New York: Dodd, Mead, & Co., 1924. Recollections of a boatman on a Colorado River survey.

Goetzmann, William H. *Exploration and Empire: The Explorer and the Scientist in the Winning of the American West.* New York: Alfred A. Knopf, Inc., 1966. Prizewinning study of western history.

Granger, Byrd H. *Grand Canyon Place Names.* Tucson, Ariz.: University of Arizona Press, 1960. Selections from *Arizona Place Names.*

Grey, Zane. *Tales of Lonely Trails.* New York: Harper & Brothers, 1922. Nonfiction adventures in the canyon country.

Henry, Marguerite, *Brighty of the Grand Canyon.* Chicago: Rand McNally and Company, 1953. Young people's classic about a Canyon burro.

Huth, Hans. *Nature and the American.* Berkeley, Calif.: University of California Press, 1957. Influence of nature on American life.

Ise, John. *Our National Park Policy: A Critical History.* Baltimore: Johns Hopkins Press, 1961. Evolution of American national parks.

Ives, Joseph C. *Report Upon the Colorado River of the West.* Washington, D.C.: Government Printing Office, 1861. An early military reconnaissance.

James, George Wharton. *In and Around the Grand Canyon.* Boston: Little, Brown and Company, 1900. Adventure, exploration and philosophy.

James, Harlean. *Romance of the National Parks.* New York: The Macmillan Company, 1939. General descriptions of national parks.

Keith, James O. *The Abert Squirrel* (Sciurus aberti aberti) *and Its Relationship to the Forests of Arizona.* Thesis. Tucson, Ariz.: University of Arizona, 1956. An ecological study.

Kolb, W. L. *Through the Grand Canyon from Wyoming to Mexico.* New York: The Macmillan Company, 1914. Exploration and river travel.

Krutch, Joseph Wood. *Grand Canyon, Today and All Its Yesterdays.* New York, William Sloane Associates, 1958. General description.

Lee, Weston and Jeanne. *Torrent in the Desert.* Flagstaff, Ariz.: Northland Press, 1962. Pictorial studies of the Colorado River.

Leydet, François. *Time and the River Flowing: The Grand Canyon.* San Francisco: Sierra Club, 1964. The views of conservationists.

MacDougall, W. B. *Grand Canyon Wild Flowers.* Flagstaff, Ariz.: The Museum of Northern Arizona and the Grand Canyon Natural History Association, 1964. Botanical list of Canyon species.

Maxson, John H. *Grand Canyon, Origin and Scenery.* Grand Canyon, Ariz.: Grand Canyon Natural History Association, 1962. Popular account of Canyon geology.

McKee, Edwin D. *Ancient Landscapes of the Grand Canyon Region.* Flagstaff, Ariz.: Northland Press, 1959. Geology of the Canyon country.

——. *The Coconino Sandstone, Its History and Origin.* Washington, D.C.: Carnegie Institution, 1933. A geological monograph.

——. *The Environment and History of the Toroweap and Kaibab Formations of Northern Arizona and Southern Utah.* Washington, D.C.: Carnegie Institution, 1938. Classical geological study of the rocks that make up the rim of the Grand Canyon.

——, and others. *Evolution of the Colorado River in Arizona.* Flagstaff, Ariz.: Museum of Northern Arizona, 1967. Theories on the geologic history of the River.

——, and Resser, Charles E. *Cambrian History of the Grand Canyon Region.* Washington, D.C.: Carnegie Institution, 1945. Geology of rocks in the lower part of the Grand Canyon.

Merriam, John C. *The Living Past.* New York: Charles Scribner's Sons, 1930. Reflections on geologic history.

Muir, John. *Our National Parks.* Boston: Houghton Mifflin Company, 1902. Poetic studies by famed conservationist.

Murphy, Thomas. *Three Wonderlands of the American West.* Boston: L. C. Page & Company, 1913. Travel descriptions.

National Geographic Society. *America's Wonderlands: The National Parks.* Washington, D.C.: National Geographic Society, 1959. General description.

National Park Service. *A Survey of the Recreational Resources of the Colorado River Basin.* Washington, D.C.: Government Printing Office, 1950. A Federal land-use study.

Nims, Franklin A. *The Photographer and the River, 1889-1890, The Colorado Canyon Diary of Franklin A. Nims, with the Brown-Stanton Railroad Survey Expedition*, Dwight L. Smith, ed. Sante Fe, N.M.: Stagecoach Press, 1967. Another view of the disastrous expedition.

Peattie, Roderick, ed. *The Inverted Mountains: Canyons of the West.* New York: The Vanguard Press, Inc., 1948. The Canyon country from several viewpoints.

Porter, Eliot. *Down the Colorado.* New York: E. P. Dutton and Company, Inc., 1969. Pictures along Powell's route.

Powell, John Wesley. *The Exploration of the Colorado River and Its Canyons.* Meadville, Penn.: Flood & Vincent, 1895; reprinted, New York: Dover Publications, Inc., 1961. Powell's narrative of his 1869 journey.

Roosevelt, Theodore. *A Book-lover's Holidays in the Open.* New York: Charles Scribner's Sons, 1916. Adventures in the Grand Canyon and elsewhere.

Scharff, Robert. *Grand Canyon National Park.* New York: David McKay Company, Inc., 1967. Guidebook.

Shelton, John S. *Geology Illustrated.* San Francisco: W. H. Freeman and Company, 1966. Rare combination of superb photos and American geology.

Stanton, Robert Brewster. *Down the Colorado.* Norman, Okla.: University of Oklahoma Press, 1965. Narrative of a railroad survey expedition.

Stegner, Wallace. *Beyond the Hundredth Meridian.* Boston: Houghton Mifflin Company, 1954. The meaning of Powell and his times.

Stockert, John W. and Joanne W. *Common Wildflowers of the Grand Canyon.* Salt Lake City, Utah: The Wheelwright Press, 1967. An illustrated guide.

Sunset Books. *National Parks of the West.* Menlo Park, Calif.: Lane Magazine & Book Company, 1970. Descriptions and photographs of major features.

Sutton, Ann and Myron. *The American West: A Natural History.* New York: Random House, Inc., 1969. The natural history of western North America.

———. *The Life of the Desert.* New York: McGraw-Hill Book Company, 1966. An ecological approach.

Terrell, John Upton. *War for the Colorado River.* Glendale, Calif.: The Arthur H. Clark Company, 1965. A short history of Colorado River battles and litigation.

Tilden, Freeman. *The National Parks: What They Mean to You and Me.* New York: Alfred A. Knopf, Inc., 1969. A philosopher's view.

Tillotson, M. R. and Taylor, Frank J. *Grand Canyon Country.* Stanford, Calif.: Stanford University Press, 1929. A ranger's view.

Ullman, James Ramsey. *Down the Colorado with Major Powell.* Boston: Houghton Mifflin Company, 1960. A young people's biography.

Van Dyke, John C. *The Grand Canyon of the Colorado.* New York: Charles Scribner's Sons, 1920. A descriptive and philosophic view.

———. *Nature for Its Own Sake: First Studies in Natural Appearances.* New York: Charles Scribner's Sons, 1917. A philosopher's study of nature.

Wampler, Joseph. *Havasu Canyon, Gem of the Grand Canyon.* Berkeley, Calif.: Joseph Wampler, 1963. A guidebook.

Waters, Frank. *Book of the Hopi.* New York: The Viking Press, Inc., 1963. Reference work on Hopi thought and culture.

———. *The Colorado.* New York: Rinehart & Company, Inc., 1946. Rivers of America series.

Watkins, T. H., and others. *The Grand Colorado: The Story of a River and Its Canyons.* Palo Alto, Calif.: American West Publishing Company, 1969. Excerpts from past writings.

Wheat, Joe Ben. *Prehistoric People of the Northern Southwest.* Grand Canyon, Ariz.: Grand Canyon Natural History Association, n.d. Early Indians of the Canyon region.

White, David. *Flora of the Hermit Shale.* Washington, D.C.: Carnegie Institution, 1929. Plant life in Paleozoic time.

Wilkins, Thurman. *Thomas Moran, Artist of the Mountains.* Norman, Okla.: University of Oklahoma Press, 1966. Biography of the famous artist.

Woods, G. K. *Personal Impressions of the Grand Canyon of the Colorado River near Flagstaff, Arizona, as Seen Through Nearly Two Thousand Eyes and Written in the Private Visitors' Book of the World-famous Guide, Captain John Hance, Guide, Storyteller, and Pathfinder.* San Francisco: Whitaker and Ray Company, 1899. Quotations.

Woodward, Arthur. *Feud on the Colorado.* Los Angeles: Westernlore Press, 1955. Battle over first steamboat navigation up the Colorado River, 1887.

Index

(Numbers in italics indicate pages on which illustrations may be found.)

231

Index

Black Mesa, 82
Black phoebe, 150
Blackbrush, 125, 139, 200
Blue grouse, 80
Blue Ridge, 32
Blue spruce, 76
Bluebell, 78
Bluebird, 45, 80
Boats, 132, 189–90
Bobcat, 25, 40, 158
Book of the Hopi, 45
Booklets, 62
Books, 62
Box canyon, 16
Box elder, 148
Boysag Point, 211
Bradley Point, 13
Brandborg, Stewart M., 175
Bright Angel Canyon, 117, 167
Bright Angel Creek, *11*, 132, 208, 210, 213
Bright Angel Fault, 94, 116
Bright Angel Point, *75*, 208
Bright Angel shale, 16, 18, 126
Bright Angel Toll Road, 216
Bright Angel Trail, 94, 116, 208, 212, 216
Brittlebush, 127, 134
Brush shelters, 146
Buckwheat, 38, 80, 134
Budget, 174
Buffer zone, 168
Bunting, 150
Bur sage, 134
Bureau of Indian Affairs, xi
Burglary, 56
Burro, 48, 118, 139, 156–57, 176, 209, 213
Butchart, Harvey, xii
Buttercup, 78, 80, 88
Butterfly, 35, 45, 88, 140, 150

Cactus, 14, 26, 45, *69*, 98, 102–03, 127, 145, 150; pincushion, 38; prickly pear, 134, 194
Cactus mice, 136
Cahn, Robert, 180
Cain, Stanley A., 204
Cairns, 117
Calcite, 152
California, 170
Calypso, 78, 200
Cambrian period, 126
Campfire programs, 22, 62
Campgrounds, 160, 167–68, 180, 184, 187–88

Camping, 178, 196
Canada, 170
Canteen, 122
Canyon de Chelly, 166
Canyon of Lodore, 130, 138
Canyon wren, 90, 112, 140, 144, 164
Cape Final, 82
Cape Royal, 72, *73*, 77, 80, 82, 89
Cape Solitude, 76, 82
Cárdenas, García López de, 46
Carrying capacity, 204
Carson, Kit, 156
Castaneda, 46
Casts, 123
Catclaw, 14, 127, 134, 148
Cathedral Stairs, 76
Cattle, 63, 158
Caves, 106, 136, 157
Celery, 152
Century plant, 35; *see also* Agave
Chaco Canyon, 44
Chat, 140, 150
Chert, 125
Cheyava Falls, 4–20, 94, 99, 136, 162, 194, 200, 210
Chickadee, 25
Chickaree squirrel, 80
Chickweed, 78
Chikapanagi Mesa, 76
Chipmunk, 24, 26, 39, 80, 88, 134, 150
Christian Science Monitor, 180
Cicero, 47
Cinder cones, 112
Cinders, 103
Clear Creek, 4, 9, 12, 13, *15*, 18, 114, 117, 210
Clear Creek Trail, 210
Cliff rose, 36, 38, 83, 88
Climate, 72, 74
Climbing, 58
Clothing, 118, 212–13
Cloudbursts, 117, 122
Clouds, 12, 41, 66, 71–72, 166, 200
Clover, 80, 88
Coconino National Forest, 51
Coconino Plateau, 82, 108
Coconino sandstone, 5, 90, 124, 140
Code of Federal Regulations, 54
Cohonina Indians, 44, 145
Colonial Williamsburg, 186, 194
Color, 39, 66, 86, 134, 142, 191, 194, 200, 222–23
Colorado, 44, 128
Colorado Plateau, vii

232

Index

235

Index

Index

Index